IN WAR AND PEACE

IN WAR AND PEACE

The Life and Times of Daphne Pearson, GC

DAPHNE PEARSON, GC

ISIS

LARGE PRINT

Oxford

First published in Great Britain 2001
by Thorogood

Published in Large Print 2003 by ISIS Publishing Ltd,
7 Centremead, Osney Mead, Oxford OX2 0ES
by arrangement with Thorogood,
the book publishing division of Acorn Magazines Ltd.

British Library Cataloguing in Publication Data
Pearson, Daphne
    In war and peace : the life and times of
    Daphne Pearson, GC. – Large print ed.
    – (Isis reminiscence series)
    1. Pearson, Daphne
    2. Large type books
    3. Great Britain – Biography
    4. Great Britain – Social conditions
    – 20th century
    I. Title
    941'.082'092

                ISBN 0–7531–9852–5 (hb)
                ISBN 0–7531–9853–3 (pb)

Printed and bound by Antony Rowe, Chippenham

"The publication of this book is dedicated to Daphne Pearson whose bravery secured the survival of our father, David Bond, who went on to build Bond Helicopters. We owe a great debt to Daphne — our very existence."

THE BOND FAMILY

The official citation in respect of Daphne's act of heroism (detailed on pages 113 and 114) reads:

On May 31 1940, an hour after midnight, an aircraft crashed near the Women's Auxiliary Air Force quarters at Detling in Kent, the pilot being seriously injured, another officer killed outright and two airmen slightly injured.

Upon hearing the crash Corporal Pearson rushed out and although she knew there were bombs on board she stood on the wreckage, roused the pilot who was stunned, released his parachute harness and helped him to get clear. When she got him about 30 yards from the wreckage a 120 pound bomb went off and Corporal Pearson threw herself on top of the pilot to protect him from the blast and splinters. She remained with him until a stretcher party arrived and then returned to the burning aircraft to look for the fourth member of the crew. She found him — the wireless operator — dead in the bomber.

The postscript on page 311 recounts how the Bond family were reunited with Daphne Pearson.

Contents

Foreword

By Air Commodore Ruth Montague
Director Women's Royal Air Force 1989–1994

When I was posted to the Ministry of Defence as Deputy Director WRAF in 1986, one of the first things I noticed, in an alcove in the Directorate, was a print of Dame Laura Knight's portrait of Assistant Section Officer Daphne Pearson, GC and I very soon had that picture hanging in my new office. Daphne's strong, intelligent, yet friendly face gave me inspiration when I felt that life was a trifle tough for me. Frequently, I wondered about Daphne because all I knew of her was that she lived in Australia, returned to the UK for the Victoria Cross and George Cross Association Reunions, and that she had been a very brave member of the Women's Auxiliary Air Force whilst serving at RAF Detling.

In May 1988, I was fortunate enough to represent Director WRAF at the VC and GC Service of Remembrance and Re-dedication at St-Martin-in-the-Fields and for the first time I met Daphne. Since then I have attended every Association Service, as DWRAF, until I retired and then as Daphne's personal guest. Daphne was such an outgoing person that, despite the huge geographical distance and the infrequency and brevity of our meetings, we became great friends. Therefore, it was with much delight that I accepted her invitation to preface this book of her life and times which has now been published posthumously.

From her childhood, as you will read, you can smell the flowers and will want to pick the vegetables; through her early career as a photographer; onwards to her time in the WRAF; then to her struggles after the Second World War in finding employment, with such variety from prisons to market gardening; and, finally, to her departure for Australia, Daphne's memories were vivid. Her writing mirrors her determination, interest in the world and the people around her, and her great kindliness that all shine from her portrait by Dame Laura Knight.

Daphne's book, in my view, will appeal to all generations. It is an excellent historical record of the earlier life of a remarkable lady, who worked in employments perhaps unusual for her times.

Ruth Montague

PART ONE

The Pre-War Years

Introduction

I think my life has been composed of taking my chance as it was offered, really to survive, but later on I was always interested in people, the way they lived and made a living from many trades and professions. Bonds were made with gardeners, artists; one looking deeper into life, the historical origins, both man-made and natural.

It is completely against my natural desires and wishes to write about myself. The first biographical approach was by a fellow-officer immediately after the war, who wrote to me and asked if she might make a film. I cannot even remember how or what I wrote but it was a definite no; I hope it was polite. I do not think it is too late to say I have been asked so often. I have my mother's letters to check on dates or locations.

I have put in a number of names of friends and of people who helped me more than they realised.

I would never have sampled life in London hotels as I did if it had not been for Margaret Black and her parents; Margaret tried to be near when needed. Dear Daphne Barnes was a very strict guide but always, to the last, a great deal of fun in spite of chronic arthritis and personal losses.

To sum up, you have my upbringing, my training, my failures, the London blitz, life in the WAAF, some life in Prison and Borstal Services. My love of plants was inborn, but I could have done more if I had studied diligently. My thanks go to my neighbours and friends near and far — there are many nicknames and surnames scattered throughout. Many of our original Detling women are living, with families.

The Navy, Army and Air Force gave its men and women good training, which was never lost in later years.

My Family and the First World War

Being born a few yards from the high tide of a lovely harbour at Christchurch, Hants, I think waters of the lakes, seas and rivers must influence a child at birth. For me this was reinforced by another home later, on an island facing the ocean for many years. For me this was a pattern of natural instinct as water is imbued into one's life — foggy, misty rain, raging seas, frothy patterns of a river eager to reach its outlet into the ocean on to a rippled, washed gulf.

Later I was a child on the Isle of Wight, twenty-six miles in circumference and home to old fishermen and sailors with rugged patient faces. We fed from the sea and from our own garden, which included chickens and tethered goats. Weekly, my mother and I fetched yellow, patterned, fresh butter from a farm nearby. There, a mug of warm milk was a treat, as I only had our goats' milk.

That was eighty years ago. I had a room of my own and, being a light sleeper, I used to sit up in bed and watch the flashes of gunfire with the distant boom, boom, from France. It was the only way of life I knew, in my home on a hill facing France with the Channel in between. There was no doubt in my mind that somehow I was going to be a sailor. Then, women were never sailors in the Navy — but this has changed sixty years later.

I remember asking Mamou, a very practical young woman who lived with us, "Does your Navy have the same uniform like us?" and Mamou replied, "In Switzerland we have not got a Navy." So out the atlas came, and I was shown where the Swiss lived; so began geography lessons, aided by my parents' stamp collections.

I began to grow up, but not alone. The house was full of people — some stayed and others were nearly permanent. There were children of parents serving overseas in Malta and Gibraltar as I remember. Wives stayed where the ship was war-based — refitting and refueling I should think; their offspring as they grew older went one by one to a mainland boarding school.

My father was a parish priest, who could not join up due to a bad left eye. The parish was much dispersed, and the main church at St Helens was a good way from the main village near the sea. We lived on top of a steep hill rising from the houses below. The Vicarage was very modern and had spare rooms for our boarders. My mother was kept very busy and also helped my father with his parish duties. He rode a black bicycle with a large leather saddlebag. Another duty he undertook was being a special constable, which gave our policeman a break. The two jobs could be combined when sometimes my father did a patrol at night.

My mother was a good organiser, a careful housekeeper and a very good cook. Now eighty years later, after reading her "book" of memories (at least the part begun before coming to the Island) I find she was rather unworldly and unsure of herself. She had seven brothers and sisters and she was the third from the bottom in age; the youngest was Aunt Grace. My mother also had two stepsisters' and one stepbrother.

I have many photographs and prints, still intact, taken by my mother. In her diary she records that my father gave her a camera to her great delight, in about 1909 or 1910. Where she could not take pictures of places or scenes, she bought the best postcard views, sometimes in sets, and many are still in good condition.

The large garden was easily organised. The postman, whose name was Coleman, delivered letters early in the morning — in those days letters were generally sparse. Coleman became our gardener after his round, and some days he had his meal with the others. The children had to call him Mr. Coleman, and in fact I never knew his Christian name.

At St. Helens I learnt a great deal about gardening and fruit and vegetable growing, and the delights of picking the fruit. Looking back, I took it for granted that if there was enough land, everyone grew asparagus, rotating beds for cutting. In the winter, especially after storms, a large cart and steaming cart-horse toiled up the hill with loads of seaweed — a great heap was made, about three loads piled up; later it was spread between the cut-down crowns in the winter. During the season asparagus was eaten for lunch or evening meals every day except Sundays, and that still left a lot to bundle up and give away. Potatoes were dug up as required. Three kinds — early, medium crops and winter ones — were neatly mounded in a stack one yard high, covered with straw and then soil on the top in case there was a frost, which was rare. The first time that I saw snow on the Island, and that was sparse, was in 1919.

Coleman was a small man with bony, deft, large hands, kindly but quite firm about the way things had to be done and when. He knew that the kitchen had to have vegetables put in the scullery and rinsed by a certain time. He never minded my probably ceaseless questions — usually on vacation time. Part of the summer-time father taught Oxford undergraduates who stayed in the house, to polish up and learn more Latin, Greek and Hebrew. These young men were Siamese, or Burmese and Indian fourth-year undergraduates. During wartime they had to get home the best they could, or remain and continue with their tutoring.

At five years old I was reading simple picture books, but later at nine, I was attending the young men's classes in Latin. My father gave me almost daily lessons in Latin so that I could catch up. French was spoken at lunchtime and during the afternoon with Mamou, and at other odd times.

From perhaps six or seven years old we would walk down to the village which consisted of a very large green, alongside green-edged, red-brick houses scattered at intervals with shops. One important one was the sweet shop run by Mrs. Trishler. She served the sweets out of large jars of humbugs, acid drops and many-coloured fruit drops. My pocket money was a penny for 10 sweets. "Stock is not as it used to be," she always said. She sold other things from the corner window.

Next-door was a haberdasher. One day my mother and I were alone and a tall, thin lady came near us peering at something. I pulled mother's arm, but I was quietly reprimanded for interrupting her purchases. In agitation I stared at the floor around the lady's feet, "But Mummy, the lady's elastic has gone — her knickers are on the floor!" I was hastily sent out of the shop and the remaining women fixed up the lady.

Chinka, pronounced by us as Chinky, was born two weeks before me. His pedigree was a cross between a Pekinese and a Sealyham, with colouring of white and big patterning of chestnut. Chinka or Chinqua is American Indian for Chestnut. His fur was long and tough. He was larger than a Sealyham and his face was like a large Pekinese with a glistening black-button nose. He was my guardian, and always slept under my pram or walked alongside when moved. No leads were used. His aggression was fearsome and hostile with rowdy boys, and he seemed to have his own rules. My parents got used to his two- or three-day disappearances — messages used to be received by my father of his sightings. He always returned, quite unrepentant and often very hungry.

Chinka was never allowed upstairs; he always slept in one of the three stables with plenty of straw near the kitchen yard, which had a stout gate that was never locked. It was to his advantage to be near the kitchen, especially in the morning when the scullery copper was lit and the kitchen range heated up. There was a large, long, coloured rug lying along the deep fender. He would sniff at the big double saucepan of real Scotch porridge simmering. Chinka was full of character and determination. He liked Mr. Coleman who represented access to the kitchen quarters. Once, he presumed to be in charge of law and order over an escaped hen — of course Chinka had connived the original havoc outside a very strong wire pen; he had his own sense of humour.

In the summer we were all very busy. There were two lawns to mow, and a fearfully long grass bank in front of the house with a pretty wide drive. Our Pompey (slang for Portsmouth) friends found a good solution — I do not know who initiated it. On a Friday a few sailors turned up and Coleman borrowed another mower. They trailed into the kitchen for a cup of tea and left bags of sugar lumps. They mowed and mowed, carefully marking the tennis courts out. Everything (nets, etc) was measured. The seamen walked singly through the side gate to the kitchen and collected baskets of currants — mostly black, some red and white — and went down to the kitchen garden entrance where a vehicle was parked. Off they went to Ryde, then over the channel by steamer to Pompey. On Saturday afternoons the officers came about 1.30p.m. and played tennis. Mother had the deckchairs out and stools for us, or a rug. Afternoon tea was served and several local ladies dropped in to entertain.

My friend Patsy from the village was with us most weekdays. Patsy and I were born just a few days apart. Her father was Army and was killed before I remember things. Patsy's mother seemed to be older than my mother, quietly remote and a bit severe. I felt we had to be very quiet and good when we had infrequent afternoon teas at Patsy's place. As I write this, Patsy has married and moved back to her original home after World War II.

In the summer we were on the beach a lot; it was quite a walk back to the Vicarage. We always had two grown-ups with us as we often collected other children. On the left of the beach near the cliffs was the treacherous "Blue Slipper". It is a blue-grey clay and, when the tide recedes, blue slipper appears from the reedy Solent channel. In the early days quite a few strangers were sucked in, and it took three rescuers with boards and ropes to prevent people being sucked down to their death. As young as we were, we knew we must watch for strangers' children to warn them.

We also had a great friend called Alec, who had meningitis when he was born in my year, from May to August 1911. It was very hot, and many children had this distressing condition. Alec was always in everything, in spite of his wiry wheel chair; he shared in some pretty rough games on the beach over the safe side near the mouth of the Bembridge River where the grown-ups had their camp, as we called it.

The river was small but swiftly flowing, and quite a few boatmen were about if the tide was right for fishing. Bembridge could have been as foreign as

Portsmouth, because we never went there, except once round by horse-drawn vehicles from the back of our small railway terminus station. Of course, the beach was our own home place to learn to swim, dog-paddling first; the littlies three to four year olds with their mothers and governesses (Mamou never swam) used to hold us in the water until we floated on our own. I don't think we were ever afraid. Angela, who lived with us, suddenly thought she would swim out on her own and cross the distant channel. I remember my mother diving in and me dog-paddling after her while she hauled Angela out from drowning.

With the incoming tide came the shrimps. Out came our shrimp nets and buckets. It was exhausting to scoop up enough for supper and for grown-ups' dinners.

When a child is small, the world that is seen is much larger than a grown-up's. When in later years a return is made to a place everything looks smaller, then the child within the grown-up says today, "I thought the place was bigger." The feature of the entrance to our home was a winding gravel drive. Gravel I have never liked since, because to earn some more pocket money I would weed out the small grasses that popped up constantly in front of the turning area. The grass seed had blown in from the grassed areas. I have disliked the dull gold of gravel ever since.

Forget-me-nots were massed through the drive rose bed. The apricot rose "Lady Hillingdon" looked pretty carpeted with blue underneath. As the flowers finished, they were barrowed out to the kitchen garden and spread in a long strip along the hedge that bordered the engine room with its gas generator (there was no electricity or telephone). Over the deadish plants light twiggy branches were laid and left until early spring. Then underneath were sturdy seedlings to plant out. There were also enough for the parish, which Coleman supervised.

Elder trees lined our lanes, and waffled along a steam-rolled, wide, ash path that led across to the village green at the far end near the railway station and the butcher. Our goats were milked at 4p.m. When I was big enough I milked one goat, and mother usually coped with one or two — it depended on nature. Other vegetables that we grew, ate and gave away were beautiful tender leeks — bleached like celery in trenches with brown paper collars; small and different cabbages — winter, spring, etc.; carrots — young spring and later the large winter ones; radishes, the children's vegetable, because that is how we were taught how to sow seeds, as they take only 10 days to germinate, with a sure result. Tomatoes were not available or hardly known unless I have forgotten.

Strawberries of course came early, with straw carefully laid under the coming fruit and fishing nets laid with small wooden pegs. "Royal Sovereign" was considered the best. Blackbirds were the usual menace. In concert, there were rows of raspberry canes, and new canes were an addition for future rows. "Lloyd George" was a type that continued on for many years in England, I believe they originated in New Zealand.

There was a row of "white" raspberries, which were in fact deep cream in colour.

The old orchard had been there before the house was built. Except for the long grass being scythed, no one seemed to bother much. There were many old varieties of fruit, including pears of some size. I remember my mother bottled and made jams for the winter from all the fruit we grew, so she had a pantry full ready for the winter — a colourful sight.

The herbaceous border was very beautiful and special to my mother. She grew this amazing colour border herself, including delphiniums of several blues, tall and very spectacular; Michaelmas daisies; Mrs. Simpkins pinks; Lychnis of scarlet or white, the usual lovely perennials. After all, flowers had to be grown for the church and at times for the village mission church that was made of tin sheets. I was a baby when it was planned. I do not remember a plant nursery. Plants were swapped and a few rare parcels arrived from "England" as I called it, as the mainland to me was the thin line of coast I could see, of which Portsmouth was the City of Ships.

There was no greenhouse but we had cold frames for seeding. Catalogues came from Sutton's and Barr's, the latter for bulbs. Skirting around the lawn areas were many flowery shrubs: Viburnums, Irish Strawberry (Arbutus unedo) trees, clumps of lilacs (Syringa), interspersed with pines and good climbing trees. I loved climbing, Chinka watching anxiously with interspersed barks. A chore, which I liked, was cleaning out the two hutches of Belgian hares (rabbits) and my favourite white rabbit with a black patch. They lived near the forget-me-not beds.

Lining the formal driveway was a clipped laurel hedge, which I hated then and still dislike. Their only use was to crush a leaf into a screw jar, in which you could anaesthetise butterflies and insects to examine them, and then look them up in a book.

The (First World) War, at my age, was a way of life: young and old men on crutches, some with bandages, others lying around on the grass or sitting in the kitchen. Mother and I went to the village on certain days when Coleman or a messenger came up — another telegram had come to Mrs. So-and-so. If father could not go at once, mother went with flowers and edibles, whatever was useful to them and at hand. I waited outside, or walked to Granny Royle and told her the bad news of another killed. So another Red Cross card was put in the window, that meant a wife or mother grieving. I remember a cottage near the mission church with four white cards with red crosses, a husband and three sons killed. At church on Sundays we prayed for those killed and missing, and for those in hospital.

I have no recollection of the day the war was over; we had no radio of course. I do not even remember church bells ringing out, perhaps there were not any, or fireworks. The most important day of peace is a complete blank. Perhaps it was a day of disbelief, and to many much grief.

I do remember during the war being told that we were going on a working holiday to Dornoch, Scotland.

The dramatic part of the train journey was going over Forth Bridge. The train came to a stop halfway. No one was to lift a blind up in case of anyone lighting a match. The Germans were overhead. We stayed there some while and a guard kept walking up and down.

My father had to take the services at Dornoch. I know we made some good friends there. I loved the whitewashed houses around the shore and wharf. Also I was made an honorary member of the Gordon clan, and allowed to wear a proper kilt. Someone gave me a sporran. There was plenty of material to lengthen as I grew! I think I may have been seven or eight years old. I never remember going back to St Helens either. It was an intended break for my parents.

Mother made all my frocks. She was interested in smocking and I had some with varied patterns. Later on she explained those that belonged to different counties, or again to different types of work in which people were employed. As a child I disliked the colour green in wearing apparel. One birthday, mother made me a very smart linen frock, light green. How hurt she was when I cried, "Mummy, you know I hate green." Worse still, I would not wear it.

Christmas time always began in October when puddings were made. Enough for presents and future birthdays. It was a ritual involving everyone. All raisins had to be strigged (have their stalks removed) and then cleansed with other dried fruits with flour being rubbed through, and sifted out in large round wooden sieves. In those days large amounts of fruit were packed in

16

blocks, straight from overseas countries. Sugar was in various-sized, blue, stiff paper bags.

Silver sixpenny pieces were scalded before being dropped into the final mixture. Everyone around stirred and wished. Then the large pans and pots were busy boiling the coarse cotton-covered basins. Later, on Christmas Eve in the early dark evening, the carol singers, some with hand bells, approached the house and encircled the porch and sang their carols; we then gave them fruit and nuts and money, put into a collection tin. With greetings and waving of lanterns they trooped away. I put out my Christmas stocking at the end of the bed, but logically I could not see how Father Christmas could come down a chimney without leaving any signs of soot! Christmas Day and Boxing Day were probably the same as in any household, with people coming in with their greetings and the exchange of gifts.

After our return from the North, my father had to go to Oxford to receive his Master of Arts degree at an encaenia being held in the Sheldonian Theatre in 1919 or 1920. Earlier he had obtained his Bachelor of Arts degree; at the time he was amongst 47 entrants and only five passed to get their M.A.! I wonder now whether he had been disadvantaged by not going to school. My great-grandparents had asked that the eldest son of my grandparents would live with them in Beverley and be tutored instead.

From what I gathered he was unhappy with his surroundings, a very large dour brick house, very solid meals and restrictions. One thing he did was to escape and join the Hull football club. He tried to avoid the heavy cooked breakfasts accompanied by porter, a dark bitter brown beer. He was always a very sparse eater, and I take after him. It must have been a great sense of relief when he was told he was going to Oxford, although he really wanted to be a policeman!

He went to Christchurch, also known as "the House". It must have been an extraordinary change in his life to be in the oldest college with a Cathedral and lovely surroundings. Because of his weakness in mathematics his tutor for that subject was the Rev. Dodgson, the Lewis Carroll of fame. I think it is generally known that every story he wrote contains a mathematical problem to be solved. Dodgson gave father a new short story with a problem, but the manuscript was stolen from his study in the Isle of Wight. Nothing was ever locked up and everyone was definitely honest over money. Father was very upset.

During the visit to Oxford, we stayed in a small hotel in The Broad (street). Mother caught a shocking cold, and was in bed for two or three days. A very nice couple staying there looked after me, whilst father was attending academic demands for the great ceremony. The weather was not good, but there were many wondrous places under cover. Near the hotel was a sweet shop and that is where I saw chocolates for the first time. Father bought a box for mother to cheer her up. Someone said the chocolate was made with coconut butter; they were awful. On the island we did not have cocoa either. One chocolate made me sick and it was not until I was in my advanced teens that I could eat anything with chocolate in it. Gradually I grew out of that.

The weather cleared up and we all attended the encaenia held in the Sheldonian Theatre. Father changed his white and black hood for a rich red one, and could add M.A. (Oxon) after his name. Mother has recounted the first time she went there, and amongst the famous names of the times was Mark Twain from the United States of America.

When returning later I could not understand why father had to have mathematics to be a policeman, or go into the civil service, or the Foreign Office. I supposed old Greek, Latin or Hebrew would not be much help.

Years before, he had married an Oxford girl, that is when my half-sister, Irene, and half-brother Reggie, were born. They both went to schools in Sherborne, Dorset; two separate buildings next door to each other. Both schools were old with nice grounds. My other cousins went there. I believe it is a very beautiful area. Reggie was an adventurous red-head always trying to climb the walls which separated him from Irene. In the end, father had to remove him and he went into the Navy. The ship he was to join was HMS *Monarch* which had sailed to Buenos Aires. Father took him to Hamburg and saw him off on to a passenger ship. Father wrote cards to my mother each day in German until he got home.

Much later, after Reggie had sent two cards en route to the Argentine, the Navy sadly told my father he was killed; he was aloft on the mainmast and fell on to the deck. Poor, poor daddy.

Irene, much older, was almost mother's age. She trained as a nurse in Edinburgh Hospital. If I became very ill, she came down and nursed me. She was tall and gentle with dark hair. Much later on, she married a very handsome surgeon of her own age. They were sent to Richmond Hospital, where Bertie was a senior surgeon. After a while, Irene went back to full-time nursing in London and Bertie went his own disastrous way. She was a sister then at St Mary's Abbott. I did not see her often. I wish I had.

The next year, my parents were getting rather mysterious and both were very cheerful. The secret was out at last; this year we were going to France for a month's exchange or locum — Father was to be priest in charge of St Malo's Anglican church to enable the present clergyman to go home or somewhere else. There was to be no visiting, just the Sunday services, and there was no Evensong. We stayed in a *pension* right near the beach. There were a number of children with their nannies and parents. I was in the care of one of them when my parents went out, explaining they caught buses going to the villages on the coast, and walked and explored. I went with them once to Mont Saint Michele.

One evening, whilst we dined, the waiter offered us American style lobster which was steamy hot with lovely gravy. For me a small serving of lobster and mother said, "Please give my daughter plenty of sauce/gravy." The waiter looked very strange and looked at me and shook his head. I said "What is the matter?" I laughed, and he went away smiling. You see the gravy/juice was almost pure brandy. Father's French was terrible and he usually shouted carefully in English. No one could cure Englishmen of this weird way of tackling this problem. I noticed when Father taught Latin or Greek, he never shouted. He was not deaf either.

On Sunday afternoons after Mass, we could do what we liked: go to the races, amusements; as there was no beach, we had an outing. Time went too quickly and we boarded the steamer to return us to Newhaven, then a train to Portsmouth, and lots of unpacking to do. Whilst away my parents let the house.

Back to the island, but whilst in Oxford our move to the mainland had been arranged, through Lincoln College in the Diocese of Oxford. We were going to Twyford, Buckinghamshire.

Buckinghamshire

July 1920. Everything was organised. I was very excited, until I learned that no animals, not even Chinka, were going. I could not imagine life without Chinka, I could always talk to him when I became lonely. Patsy was preparing to go to school, I have forgotten where. The two Dublin cousins, Mary One and Mary Two, were returning to Dublin. They did a lot of cleaning and helped in the kitchen; they were so alike, they could have been sisters. Chinka quietly vanished; he had gone to his old holiday haunts.

I was absorbed into the pattern of grown-up meals. I missed the Irish Mary's potato cakes in the nursery. Life was full of queries — would the river be as exciting as the sea? We were leaving the sea with all its moods, beautiful colours and boats, for unknown rivers, ponds and different scenery — another world. I knew it was much colder with snow in the winter.

But Chinka was my main worry. Chinka silently vanished forever. He knew this was not a normal holiday, seeing the arrival of the removal vans. I vainly hoped he would return to say goodbye, but he was never seen again; later father wrote to the island but he had gone. I do not remember anything distinctly, I was sad yet excited — steamer, train and another train were a new experience.

We were only at Twyford for three years; much happened in that time. It was a small village, but covered a large parish containing two hamlets within a triangle. A railway crossed the land, passing near the house, not many trains went through the scattered farms. There were well-kept hedges and the carefully placed, fully grown hawthorns, which in hunting terms are called bullfinches when set in a ditch.

The church was at the far end of the road, where cottages and a few shops mingled and finished with the blacksmith, near the lych gate entrance to the church, which was very old with a square tower. I always felt it to be a cold church, very solid, with brasses set on the graves under the solid stone floor. The Vicarage was very close behind the church. A broad path led to a small entrance side gate, passing by very old gravestones. There was a tall Berberis on the left with shining green leaves, wicked spines protecting the orange flowers which later on turned into brilliant red fruit. Past that was the house — a low, long Elizabethan dwelling, full of history, well proportioned, facing east, a sizeable long lawn lined with tall elms. There were several gaps in the line that allowed the view of a large field, and let in the morning sun which lit up the old mellow bricks.

At the back of the house was a drive lined with old lime trees, with very pretty light green leaves, leading past a small lodge which was being repaired. There was an old neglected orchard, and a field by the entrance on the far side. Then an enclosure with ducks and chickens, opposite a stable with a high loft with bales of hay. Alas, no pony yet.

The back door was large and old, not as big as the front door that was heavily studded; through both doors there were steps to go down. The whole ground floor had solid large slabs of worn stone. From the front door turning left, the hall took up the width of the house, with mullioned windows facing each other. One then entered the drawing room: a large fireplace and three windows with set-in seats, which had a view of the flower border, and a well kept large garden, fruit and vegetables and back view of the mature lime trees, and near view of the church tower.

The study was built on top of the stone floor, so it was cosy with a wooden floor; if you turned right there was a very beautiful curved Jacobean staircase, which attracted some historians who wrote and asked to examine it.

Wandering left down the passage, a dining room was next to the spacious kitchen. A Mr. and Mrs. Whitcher had arrived, who both in the past had worked for Granny Benson, my mother's mother. They were country people from Worcestershire and could overcome anything. Mrs. W. seemed very pleased with the huge range in the kitchen; she was not young but seemed a large person with strong arms, and very cheerful.

Another historical and unique feature of the house was the roof with its original tiles, but re-set later to allow gun barrels to be sited through holes at irregular places, for the Royalist soldiers who were hidden in the attic — over 50 of them. There were many skirmishes and battles fought in the district. Upstairs, my parents had a large room at the north end of the house, near the poultry menagerie and the drive end. To get to it one had to go up four or five steps and through another room, their dressing room, which also had a bed in it. Returning down the steps was a large bathroom which had been a bedroom, and next was the lavatory. Then, round the top of the polished old banister led into a passage, very dark wide oak floor planks which were shining, and at the side a small original powder room, where wigs were adjusted in olden days. Then a long bedroom, spare room, the passage had long windows facing the elms. Then up three or four steps, a set to the right side room and the set to the left, my room. A thick creeper (it may have been a trained ornamental pear) came up to the sill, which was very important because I later had a very intelligent cat that climbed up to be let in. She was supposed to be in the stables!

The next room was occupied by a young woman who did a mixture of work, especially in the evenings, as the Whitchers slept out.

As a child, I was busy exploring but I was very lonely. The local people were very solid, not tall, but I suppose they were descended from a hard life on the land, and the women had suffered war losses. I know father had to have guest curates because one hamlet, Charndon, grew larger because of an expanding brickworks. Trains were both freight for the bricks, and some were passenger trains for Oxford. We had no car, but an elderly man had a trap, which took four people to the station.

So in those years I began music lessons again, in Oxford with Miss Brain, who lived in a row of houses adjacent to Worcester College where my grandfather and my Great Uncle George went. It is away from the town centre, but near many colleges. We walked through the Quads (quadrangles) until there was a lake of some size, and adjacent pastures and trees with quite a few seats. The lake has many water birds, including various kinds of ducks. Groups of flowering plants according to the season. This garden had been built by a Bursar. Worcester was one of the original colleges of student monks from Benedictine abbeys, the first cell was founded in Oxford in 1283, the surviving buildings are still intact. The northern yew-clad terrace is still called Monks' Walk.

At home, I had to practice on the piano at least an hour a day, but my education had to be overhauled I suppose. Then something happened over father's health; it was arranged that the Lonsdales who lived in the second hamlet, Poundon, were going to look after me for some weeks or months until father was better. There was a small church in Poundon where services on certain Sundays had to be taken. So began a very, very different life in a very large house with extensive grounds, gardens, tennis courts, woods, fields and stables with hunters and all the accompanying necessities to support a medium-size estate. The owner was the Master of the Bicester Hunt, he and his wife had two children, Mary was probably fourteen and the son, Charles, a cheerful and fun-loving child of seven or eight years. A tall and gifted governess reigned supreme, with kindly firmness, in a large schoolroom with a long table and tall windows on two sides.

We three had different grade lessons. Latin was not taught. My arithmetic was about Charles' standard, and my English, history, drawing and spelling were nearly up to Mary's form. We had a room each, which was on the first floor, past several large bedrooms where there was a small night nursery, where we had some evening meals and hot drinks before bed. We had lunch in the dining room, unless there were guests of importance. Depending on the number of people, two footmen used to be in attendance. The butler was in charge of all the domestic staff; he was much liked by everyone. As children we always called him "Mr. B.", grown-ups called him by his surname only. Our good manners towards the servants, including grooms and gardeners, were very strictly enforced.

Most afternoons we walked, and were taught names of plants and encouraged to learn how things were done. Mary shone out as an exemplary hostess if visitors were about, and sometimes was taken off to official visits.

When the winter was upon us, the hunting season began in earnest. The first meet was at the house. Mrs. Lonsdale and Mary rode sidesaddle and looked immaculate; both had good looks. Trays of hunting cups of wine and/or spirits were handed round before taking off. The hounds were impatient for the ritual to begin. At the end of all the hunters, Charles and I, with a few youngsters on ponies, went for about half a mile or so where the hunt peeled off to pick up a scent of a fox, pink coats rushed on and over the hedges and ditches. I went to an early cubbing one frosty morning, barely dawn. I felt that was very cruel but I suppose I accepted it.

When spring came, plovers' eggs were gathered off tufts of tussocks where the birds neatly laid up to four eggs on the flattened centre; we always left one or two, and moved off to another area next time. These were a luxury, put out hard-boiled in bowls on the dining room table at lunchtime.

Father used to come up sometimes with mother to Poundon to take a morning service. I think the car used to fetch them. It was strange to say goodbye to them; I missed my mother very much. They were asked to lunch but father had to do the Children's Service in the afternoon.

When there were large dinner parties, we were allowed to watch the guests below, from the balcony landing, as they arrived. We had a nursery maid with us to control our excitement. We watched the beautifully dressed people as their coats were taken away, the butler announcing their names; some guests looked up and waved.

Sometimes Mary used to come with me to the Vicarage in the afternoon. We usually walked. She liked rambling around over the railway lines and across the stream with its rather shaky bridge. In spring the wildflowers were miraculous: orchids and fritillaries, stichworts, and primroses.

By the spring I had returned to the Vicarage. I began certain lessons at Claydon village where our doctor lived. His daughter was a teacher so I went on with French, and my impossible arithmetic lessons. Then one day returning on Stella, the cob, we met a steamroller. Stella got the bit between her teeth and tore past the steam dragon. I hung on for two miles until I jerked her to a halt outside her stable. I was furious and scared but as I slid down the Doctor had followed and came out of his car; he smiled, handing me my whip with the two black ribbons off my pigtails, and my white scarf. A farmer had phoned him from somewhere.

I rubbed Stella down and fed and watered her. I had to go three and a half miles to my lessons and be back by 4p.m. every Tuesday. The cob, Stella, belonged to the butcher. She had a white blaze and was a chestnut. His shop was off the village street, and the stable was almost built on to our field.

One day going over the stile from there, I was faced with a fox with our favourite and largest drake in his mouth. I tore into him with my whip and sadly gathered up the drake and his torn beautiful feathers. Country life was often tough and sad. Another incident happened near the stable which shocked me into fury and horror seeing a group of boys on the side of the road laughing at a squirming, fluffy tabby kitten. They had a hay fork and were trying to pin it down between the two prongs. As I tore into them, they'd missed, its insides trailing out. It was a tabby kitten with its white fur turning red. I know I yelled, screamed and hit and

29

hit them, until there was a silence and the butcher came out and held me while I cried. I was told afterwards their parents were told to deal with them. I learned that children of my age were capable of anything, especially boys. Thus, a fox kills for food and family. Some humans kill and torture for fun, so as I did my history, reading included tales of the Royalists and Roundheads fighting and destroying families who may have played together in childhood. Nightmares come to us all emanating from witnessing life in the raw.

Next day was a Wednesday. We went by train to Oxford and continued my music lessons with Miss Brain. Later we went up into the main town for tea and iced coffee at the Cadena, and on through the covered market and Sainsbury's, famed for its bacon, meat and cheese delicacies. Then to another college, usually Christchurch, known as "The House" where father used to go.

The next change to come upon us was my mother's mother Granny Benson and my youngest aunt coming and staying with us permanently. Granny could only move slowly from her bed to her chair. The two of them shared the largest long bedroom. The fire was always lit early; in those days there were many paraffin black round stoves about three and a half feet high, a common sight at the time. They gave out good heat, but had to be filled, and the wicks trimmed daily. Another chore that took time.

The Whitchers had settled in and as the household grew, Mr. Whitcher used to help with the range in the kitchen, cleaned windows and did semi-outdoor work.

A choirboy called Jimmy helped before school; he was 12 years old and the head of a large family, his father was killed at the end of the war. Jimmy arrived very early and began cleaning the boots and shoes, on the left of the back door were various workplaces, laundry and pantries. Jimmy had his routine, and before he left for school, Mrs. Whitcher gave him a good cooked breakfast, and sometimes gave him notes to deliver. The school and chapel were at the opposite end of the village.

The most interesting cottage industry was lace making. I spent one or two afternoons a week with an old woman who taught me the rudiments. Sometimes mother went by train to Buckingham, or in a friend's car, and bought our lace pillows and stands. I had to start on a small-width Bucks pattern. Setting up a pillow was very complicated. The bobbins that were not used were kept in a bobbin box locally made by the men folk. For practical use and speed, my mother made Torchon lace with straighter lines and wider width. I think she went with friends sometimes to lectures and demonstrations, either to Olney, a great centre for lace, as well as Buckingham. The bone bobbins were made by sailors to while away the time overseas. They cut names and brief messages to their wives and sweethearts, i.e. "to Mary, my love", and so on; they bored shallow holes and filled the holes with red paint to stand out.

The lace pins had two different-coloured heads; red sealing-wax knobs for special places in a pattern; when the Goosegrass seeds were gathered, one pushed the head of the pin into the green seed, the knobbed pin was crowned and hardened in a few days and turned black.

Before going on to our next home near Oxford, my father had always been troubled by one eye, which had only dim vision. In those days, nothing medically could be done for the clot behind the eye. This sometimes made him accident-prone. One morning in his study there was a fearful crash. A bookcase along a wall from the window loosened and fell on his head. That did not help his vision and then, when he was resting and patched up, he looked so forlorn, I wished he could have a car like other people that visited, the doctor, farmers and well-off clergy.

If it wasn't daddy in the wars it was me with my colds and coughs — the mustard poultices and the inhalations were an added nuisance to everyone. There must have been a lot of discussion with the authorities so he was given the parish of Combe, near Oxford, which was partly in the Cotswolds and at a higher altitude.

Granny was neither better nor worse. She was just old, gentle, perceptive, and Aunt Grace was very good. She went stone-deaf after measles when she was 12 years old. She could lip-read and she used to laugh at our mutual mistakes. I cannot remember when we parted, where they went, I think it was outside St Albans where the family had long-time friends named Pearce. The Whitchers eventually returned to be near their son. Granny would have missed her cooking; she knew all the simple dishes that she liked. Sometimes when I went to bed, I sat on a stool beside Granny and she used to cut off a tidbit which she'd give me with a gleeful smile. She would have been quite tall, like many of the family she reared. So to our next home.

PART ONE

The Pre-War Years

Combe and Oxford

Combe, also Long Combe, and in latter years Coombe, was under the auspices of Lincoln College, Oxford. The Vicarage was a redbrick house, much smaller than the last. Ugly, I thought, but much easier to live in and for father to walk out of a side door, across the lawn and up to the entrance door of the church, which was very old and beautiful, 14th century.

The village was attractive; all the houses, made of the soft-coloured Cotswold stone, were sited within a large triangle of a spacious village green. On one side was a huge oak tree. There were two pubs, one on each side of the other roads; their customers were grouped distinctly by occupation. The road that went past the Vicarage and quite a few small houses, with quite large kitchen gardens swung round the group containing Freddy Putt's Bakery, and opposite him was his sister's Post Office and their home. Our large Lebanon cedar at the beginning of the small lawn and adjacent to our front gate was very old but had many years to go. Its branches stretched over the large village well, sited in another triangle of grass by the fence. Across the road and in a very large field was a big pond, which usually had a few ducks on it, but it was in private property.

34

The school was small and belonged to the Church of England but was attended by all denominations. On Tuesday, Father gave a lesson in religious instruction which did not offend the Wesleyan Chapel-goers' children. The people of Combe were more outgoing, and seemed to get together in good humour. They liked singing together. A good half of the parish worked for the Duke of Marlborough. The south gate of Blenheim Palace Park was in Combe. Outside the gate was a large orchard in which was planted the delicious "Blenheim Orange" apple, dessert or cooking with its red flush and red and russet stripes. Locally it was THE Christmas apple — its fault was sometimes its huge squat size.

On Wednesdays we had a local bus which stopped outside the back gate, where there was a large gravel area. The bus went to and from Oxford all day, as it was market day. The cattle market was very near the Oxford railway station, the indoor market was undercover, in the centre of the town; there was a café of sorts, all fruit and vegetables and homemade items were displayed.

So it meant we could continue my piano lessons, until the next upheaval. This time it meant half an hour's practice a day. It meant, too, more time to see the colleges and the gardens. We could go to the early Evensong at 4p.m. at the Cathedral in Christchurch; the choirboys were from the college school so they sang every Wednesday. We could have plenty of time to walk to the railway station and the cattle market to pick up a bus.

Our lunch walks were to St. John's (College) in the spring, which has very beautiful rock gardens and seats under and near willow trees, and Magdalene (College) and its lovely walks round the deer park and the Cherwell River. There was Trinity (College) to find the ancient large turtles, and Blackwell's bookshop with its myriad passages of books nearby.

When we moved into the Combe Vicarage, we eventually had a young woman from Somerset, after a disastrous start in the domestic scene with a discharged prisoner with an excellent reformed reputation. He was a very correct and courteous man and was a very good coach for cricket, but he was caught on his day off in Oxford stealing money, apparently that was his main achievement. Then Gladys arrived from Somerset, she had the attic rooms with nice views, she was helped on Mondays and any very busy days by someone from the village.

Mother had her Mothers' Union meetings in the dining room every month and Girls' Friendly Society meetings; she often teamed up with adjacent parishes to go on a hired bus to Reading for cheese classes. This was very successful; her aspiration to make cheese began in France, St Malo. She made hers on straw mats, they were like a mild Brie, very good indeed. One or two people caught on and asked for classes in other things, the villagers were much more outgoing.

Father was very surprised over the church bells, which had fallen through the belfry many years before due to a fire, and no one had the energy to raise funds or care. He planned their restoration meticulously. The bells were resting in Taylor's Foundry at Loughborough where they were originally cast. He must have done quite a bit of lobbying in Oxford, because he began coming in on the second bus on Wednesday and, as he was a life member of the Union (a society for all university members) he could meet people there: historians and people with money, probably our two bishops. It was always men only then, except for the Ladies' Room.

But at 4p.m. mother and I turned up, there was a large typical men's room for entertaining ladies, tea at 4p.m. We did not do this often because we began to be busy shopping for the church and various events to raise money. Father wrote a good appeal in *The Times* and then printed out at certain intervals how much had been collected and what was needed in other publications. He wrote a number of personal letters.

Eventually the bells were restored, tuned and peeled out. Then they were silent until the Bishop of Oxford and his Suffragen Bishop blessed the bells. Some of the original bell-ringers taught others. Every Tuesday was practicing evening. All the different changes were practiced. Extra nights had to be booked because the young men had to be taught. It was so rewarding, that after all the years father had achieved something by himself.

At School and Training

At sometime I was told I was going to school in Clacton-on-Sea. I had a shocking cold, and I had missed ten days of term. I felt very forlorn. The girls were quite nice but apparently if you were good at a subject you were put into a form quite high up, and if you were very poor you went below your form. As I have said before, I was no good at arithmetic and had never seen algebra or geometry so I really began at the bottom. I was in much higher classes for French, Latin and drawing. The cold was intense and it was getting near the end of term, then I was so ill that I could not speak. Term was over and I tried hard to tell them; they eventually sent a telegram to Combe. A nurse kept saying we must get a doctor. Next day my sister Irene arrived, I was overcome. She insisted on getting the doctor and told him she would get an ambulance to London and then transfer me home. Soon we were on the way. I next realised I was in my own room, with a fire. Irene slept in the spare room next to mine. She had taken special leave from the hospital.

When I was well enough, I had to take an oral examination and a small written one in Oxford to satisfy the new school to which I was going in Bristol. A very well run school, but very strict; about one-third of the girls were Welsh and spoke their language nearly all the time. They all had some musical excellence, piano, voice or strings. Violin, viola or cello was an extra. On the whole I did not like school at all. The place was so dark and dreary, with large elms on the terrace with sooty black trunks.

Our playing fields were four miles away by tram, so we trundled out there every Saturday for cricket in the summer and hockey. That was good. Netball and tennis were played at the school itself. We swam in the Public Baths over the hill usually on Tuesdays and Fridays; the water was freshly changed before we were there at 7a.m. Swimming was compulsory; Life Saving Drill was carried out unexpectedly in the Great Hall. I was not enthralled with walking two and a half miles down through the docks to Templestowe to our church and doing the same in the evening; the latter I avoided when I could. In the summer that was easy, I found some good places to climb and sketched views over the city; we were very high up. I had no special friend. The little spare time we had, I spent in the library. It was quiet and usually empty. Some of the early books were very interesting and hardly read. I enjoyed my drawing classes. I hated practicing the piano in one of the cells; a corridor of upright pianos, a numbered list of names with times of practice went up daily. One felt claustrophobic.

A practice, which was instilled into me as the right thing at home, as the right thing was the privacy of letters belonging to other people, which was also accorded to oneself. It was just not right to read other people's letters, unless invited to or given to read. We had to sit in a class-room to write home on Sunday afternoons and hand the letter up with envelope written to the mistress in charge; she would check the envelope and handwriting and settle down to read your letter, and say "re-write that" or "leave that out". Every letter was censored and she had lists of all our names, so no one was ever allowed to complain. I am amazed and appalled at what was accepted by parents. I never told mine, they had enough to cope with.

In the classroom I was next to a very nice girl Betty McKay, who was Scottish and lived with her aunt all the time. Her father was a Colonel in the Indian Army, and she would see him perhaps every three or four years. I think her mother was dead. Both our birthdays were on the same day in May. She was tall and athletic: first team for netball, running-up for a place in tennis against our V and VI formers. They were grown-up in their seventeen and eighteen years, and knew where they were going and did outside exams. Betty was a quiet achiever and an excellent swimmer; she got her bronze then her silver in swimming.

We all had tuck boxes from home at the beginning of term. We could add to our box, at least our parents did for special occasions such as birthdays. A few of us were left in the school at half term and birthdays. The Welsh had scuttled over the border to Wales. We had no-one to visit us, so we enjoyed ourselves the best we could, walking up and down the terraces or banked garden if fine, play something or practice, but not the gym because of safety. Betty, the Scot, always gave a faint smile or nodded, to decide what to do. She turned up in my life in the Air Force, much, much later on — quiet, immaculate — and then vanished somewhere. We always met in London by chance, and she shared my friends for a few days. Betty McKay was not in sympathy with the authority over censorship of personal letters either in school or later on in the Forces.

Some of my holidays were shared. The Rector of Lincoln College had a family (Munro family) consisting of Isabel, the eldest, who was leaving college (Oxford) and had majored in Classics, including modern history; Helen, who had studied Art and was becoming known as a very promising sculptor, she had a very good eye for figures and head portraits; Hester, who was my age, a very quiet and reliable person, but she had not shown any inclination to be anything, which depressed her; and Alec.

Hester used to say to me, "My family including my parents are very gifted and know exactly what they wanted to be, except perhaps Alec." Alec was the youngest and still at school. He was very busy with his sport and friends and had no fears of the future. Hester was still at High School. She stayed with us, sometimes for three weeks or long weekends. I used to stay two weeks in Oxford in college rooms opposite Lincoln after Christmas. There were a few parties, a pantomime and so on.

Hester was taller than I and very pale, she thought she might be a nurse; she was very practical but very shy and sometimes remote. She enjoyed our picnics and bike rides in the countryside. I felt she was a very reliable and solid person. That is how, long after when everyone had broken away, if ever I was in trouble I always knew I could go to Lincoln College for help.

Looking back at school, we never had any unpleasantness over stealing, because there was none. That was one good thing. The school was on the edge of a public open space surrounding John Cabot's Tower; where you climbed and climbed up inside to the top, the stone balustrade around had been inserted with a brass with all the points of the compass, and every capital city was engraved on the arrows. I always pointed out proudly to Sydney and said my Uncle Charlie lived there when he was not sailing the China Seas to Shanghai, down to Hong Kong and Darwin. There were four or five of the Bibby Line Ships containing freight of value, and I think (I am guessing) perhaps 40-60 passengers. Uncle Charlie was my mother's favourite brother: he and his family lived in Liverpool, the Bibby Line's homeport.

To this day, I have a large dark boomerang from the Northern Territory which he gave me. He warned me not to throw it as it might kill someone when it bounded back.

This term was the final one for taking the Oxford School Certificate, a series of exams in the subjects we had studied. If we had 50 marks or over it was a pass. To have matriculation one had to pass in mathematics, and with matriculation you had your entrance to any university and other business openings. I got four per cent in arithmetic.

It was the end of my last term, the finish of schooling for me, and many others. I travelled from Bristol's Templestowe Station, very dreary, dingy and smoky, and low-lying beyond the docks amidst huge warehouses. Our luggage and boxes were neatly stacked in the order of our destinations, for quite a few the first stop Swindon, all change for Oxford. There my parents met me and we took the local train to Handborough and a taxi took us to Combe.

I was not good enough for the Slade School of Art, I knew that four out of six of my drawing exams were reasonable but my work was not "of excellence". The goal was 70 per cent plus. It was arranged that I should go to G. Methven Brownlee's Photographic Studio as a pupil — on trial to see if I had an aptitude and fitted in — which in the end was a very good opening, and I was thrilled to learn a new means of expression. So arrangements were made.

I had three changes in living out; the first one was a disaster, a Miss Russell, tall and a real sour sort of person and a dark depressing house. No cheer, no smiles; she kept saying, "my father was a judge who used to say ..." I shall never forget the food, the prunes and blancmange, watery cabbage and so on. In the end, when I knew the ropes and was part of the studio, I used not to return there until 10p.m. Then mother was given an address of a widow with two sons, a Mrs. de Vaux. Her first lodger was a young woman who was full of energy, the first woman racing-car driver, also a young man Gerald; we had excellent food for breakfast and dinner. Also it was a good-sized, sunny house. We all went off on our various ways to work. I always walked; it saved money but not shoe leather!

I began in the studio's large workroom, where the prints were mounted and put in their piles, then into crisp folders. When the negatives came from the darkroom, they were put into transparent envelopes with corresponding numbers and taken to the retoucher; Brownie then came round to discuss those to be discarded and those to be proofed on daylight paper for consideration further. The images came through quickly and were put into black envelope cases; then chosen for the final print proofs for the customer's choice.

A dear person called Elsie, who had been in the workroom for years, was a hunchback. She had dark curly hair, a wide smile and was kind and helpful. She organised the tea breaks, and took batches of work around to the right machines or tables. A very serious stocky boy called Bernard did the cleaning and deliveries. The entrance to the studio was in a side road off Park Street, near the top. Slanting across was the new University of Bristol with a wonderful tower. As one went in to the studio on the left were steps down into the First Edition bookshop owned by Douglas Cleverdon, who was a publisher of fine books, and who also had an old and very distinguished printing machine. One then went upstairs. The place was a 17th-century building, stairs wound up to The Clifton Arts Club on the left, which opened on to a stage and hall. The main entrance was on the other side. We wound upstairs again with now elegant wooden handrails into a very pleasant spacious room with several windows and a highly polished wooden floor with colourful rugs. A large old polished table with more large rugs around was the reception area. Flowers were in bowls on the large window spaces. If a client came to be photographed, curtains were drawn at the end of this area. There were hidden screens of linen, black velvet or matt oatmeal weave and so on rolled down, whichever was chosen. Brownie did all the operating, but she did have a partner for certain people. Her name was Audrey Pearson. She was tall, had fairly short, black, straight hair, and wore mannish shirts, collars and cuffs and well cut skirts. She also did some work of her own. She had a very nice house in Clifton, where on some occasions I had an evening meal, and I saw her very good work: so different. Brownie was often away and Audrey took over and was very efficient and strict. Right beyond the working areas, a door led to a flat where Douglas, Brownie and a waif called Wilfred or Wilf lived.

When I had settled in to some sort of routine — I was the only pupil — I did quite a bit of reception work. Gradually, I learned the secrets of the darkroom, and was entrusted to make up fresh chemicals as required. In hindsight, there was so much to do because there was a periodical urgency for the photographing of theatre work. Some new plays were shown for a week or so, prior to official openings in London. Adjustments were made and publicity involved taking a lot of pictures. Sometimes I was allowed to go down to the theatre at 10p.m. with Brownie. Scenes were shot after the main rehearsals; also the star performers were enticed for sessions into the studio. Brownie was very well known, she had many friends and her portraits were unique.

A momentous occasion was the new opera, *The Immortal Hour*, by Rutland Boughton. It was to be a Royal Command opening night in London. Rutland was an old friend of Brownie's, very genial and full of life. A fascinating fortnight followed. Rutland had a huge family of children, who all came with him; his second wife was looking as if she would have a child any minute, she was the daughter of a bishop. Her great friend was his first wife who was caring for her; also a mutual friend was Rutland's current mistress. One very cold Sunday, we put up tables and chairs from the Arts Club which filled the length of the reception area and the studio, for a tea party. Brownie was a skilled provider; but alas, living on nothing was a worry in a monetary sense, and yet people gave her enormous credit because she always paid in the end or when she could. Being in such a prominent place in Park Street, she could choose the best from all kinds of provender's. So the children tucked in and thoroughly enjoyed it all. The pictures of *The Immortal Hour* were memorable. So were the write-ups from London after the troupe went from Bristol (the Princess Theatre) to the great opening which was a Royal Command.

Another character that absorbed me was Eric Gill, the artist, sculptor, author and philosopher. Eric would be staying in Clifton, and on Sundays he invited me to Mass at a church which had a beautiful organ. He wore a long brown robe and sandals, he was very tall. He was organising parts of his sculpture to be photographed before being put together in Westminster Cathedral — the Stations of the Cross — which are a great feature today. His unique family came over for a few days or a week, usually singly. His daughter Petra was a gifted artist, and his son-in-law was David Tegetmeier. David, as Editor, was assembling the first Roman Catholic dictionary. He gave me a woodcut "Black-eyed Susan".

He used to say to me that one day I would meet the right sailor! In my spare time I used to haunt the docks to see the various ships, and found large niches in the stonewalls and broad steps up to the loading bays. Some of the chains and rings are still there to which the slaves were attached prior to 1838.

I kept my eye open in nearby streets with small dingy shops that had second-hand books, 6d. each. I once found a pristine leather-bound volume of a famous poet — a first edition. Douglas gave me £25 for it. Later, in a private dining room belonging to someone to whom I was asked to leave a letter and wait for an answer, I saw a scarce first edition of *Alice in Wonderland*. I asked the lady of the house if I could look at it, and there was all the evidence. As I put it back amongst a lot of very ancient schoolbooks I said, "May

47

a friend of mine look at that book please?" She assented, looking puzzled, and I left. Douglas rang her, and immediately went up to see her. The book was without a fault or tear, a mint first edition. He offered her several hundred pounds. Swiftly she said, "I will think about it." She sent it to one of the London auctioneers where she had to pay commission and insurance. But for Douglas she would never have known. Douglas said I could have given her £20 and she might have sold it to me. Honesty hardly pays sometimes. I liked, and still do, to find scarce books in odd places.

I was leading a life full of colour and surprises. The Clifton Arts Club was a very interesting meeting place for exhibitors of paintings and playwrights. An annual event was held during two weeks of evenings of three one-act plays, written by amateurs and professionals. They competed against other groups throughout the country. A team of well known, erudite judges adjudicated at each performance. The stage was not large, but we had good props and a storeroom; the whole area was over the bookshop and under the floor beneath the studio and all its rooms including the living areas.

Historically, this building with its old timbers and atmosphere had a past embodied in the present. Yes, there was a ghost; she was seen several times by Brownie who said she was a very sad woman searching for something. I cannot remember all the details now, but sceptics can research this in the Bristol libraries. When a bomb demolished the building in the 1940s and by fire, the local paper gave it great prominence, and recorded its history centuries back and the authentic people who had seen the mourning figure. I will admit that when I looked after Wilf some evenings, whilst Brownie and Douglas were out, I used to walk quietly through the living areas, the workroom and to the studio with its large stage curtains drawn back, and gaze down towards the moonlit windows. I was fearful, yet eager, to meet this inhabitant of several hundreds of years. Although I had some religious beliefs, but not others, I cannot say truthfully that I do not believe in ghosts. At the studio entrance door from the road a big frame hung outside with just one recent portrait. A striking one was of Joan Hart, actress and singer, with her flared bright red hair and her blue eyes lightened up. Prints were made on Kodak or Ilford deep cream paper, which gave them a distinguished low-key warm brown colour.

Once, after I became a fixture, Douglas was away and there was no one to go on the tram (the stop was nearby) with the post to the GPO for the midnight clearance to London. Brownie had no one, and was loathe to ask me. I laughed and said, "It's quite safe, both going and coming, the tram stops outside the Post Office." Once I took three packages and luckily, also my squash racquet. As I was going back to my lodgings, I turned round from the post box and a huge fellow in the middle of the pavement leered and made a dive at me. There was not a soul about but I heard a tram in the distance. I faced him and like a flash drove the head of my racquet into his solar plexus, and was amazed when he fell smack on the back of his head on the hard pavement. I shall never know if I killed him and I never told Brownie or anyone the next day. I crossed the tramlines to hop on to an approaching tram and was glad there were quite a few workers in it.

By this time I was lodging with a Miss Cox who was very elderly but spry and homely. She was such a dear, she drew like an angel and her watercolours were exquisite. She had hung her work all the way up the steep stairs. A gallery of small Baxter's prints and many smaller engravings were at the top of the landing, a veritable treasure-house from her old home. We were near some public swimming baths, so I could hop over in my togs and have a swim before breakfast in the warmer days. "Coxy", as my landlady was affectionately called by the artists around, was a full supporter of the Clifton Arts Club, she admired James Floyd's paintings and was glad I had made friends with him on a casual basis. We were great friends even though James was 22 years older than me. We would discuss the pictures that were hung; little did I know that our lives were to be much criss-crossed in and out until he died in 1955. Later I wrote a small summary of his life when he died:

James Francis Murray Floyd was born on 5 March 1889 in Kensington, and educated at Clifton College and Queen's College, Oxford (B.A. in 1911), later Glasgow University. He served in France until 1918. In the twenties he joined a zoological expedition, exploring the Amazon for four years with William Beebe, explorer and zoologist, now a director of the New York Zoological Gardens. Floyd, a qualified entomologist, had been commissioned to collect for Edinburgh University.

From childhood, his interests were in natural history and drawing, and in 1927 his paintings were exhibited in the Beaux-Arts Gallery. Also, for many years he was a prominent exhibitor in the West Country, including the Bath Society of Artists. He lived near Bath at one time, and later in the Wye Valley. Finally he moved to Cuckfield, before serving in the Home Guard and Royal Artillery in World War II.

For weeks he used to travel through France and Holland on his bicycle, painting. His thorough knowledge of birds and insects make his studies informative as well as decorative. Accurate observation, detailed notes in his dairies, and innumerable drawings embrace a wide field in fauna and flora. He was influenced by the French Impressionists and had a great love of brilliant colour. Although apt to be a recluse, he enjoyed the company of young people, and many a child was enriched with a drawing lesson, a pet or plants to cherish.

He died in his sleep on 1 November 1955 at the age of 64 at Cuckfield, Sussex, England. His drawings and paintings are stamped Floyd Atelier.

The present chairman of the Club was Donald Hughes, who had a rather flamboyant style of painting; he had a charming wife who wore Spanish shawls and had dark hair and beautiful eyes. They were both gifted; Donald published verse in booklets. They were much liked and freely gave invitations to visit. Donald was born in Wales, the same as Douglas Cleverdon. He was always kindly, reliable, and later, as you will see, directed my life into quite another sphere.

For a brief time I attended art classes in the evening. It was difficult to make it regularly because I had so much to learn in photography. One thing at that time was the explosion of modern thinking and expressions in various forms of art. The first exhibition of some magnitude was in England, in Bristol, the French Impressionists. James showed me his favourites. People came from everywhere; it caused much discussion in the Press. I could only go once because it was a very expensive admission.

Many other events cropped up. It was suggested that I was to have a "coming-out" party, as I was to be 18 on 26 May. My parents came down to stay at a small commercial hotel in Park Street. Two of the Club members offered to play de Falla on two pianos, plus some fun things; it was a mini-concert, scattered around dancing and some good plates of simple food. Someone gave a case of red wine, others cider, beer, coffee, tea, soft drinks, and everyone clubbed in for real champagne. I was very touched: I think I was the youngest of the Club. My practical role was noises off and imitating trains with various sized bottles and whistles when the plays were performed. I was given a list of sounds required. I gathered a lot from the backstage theatre folk. I used the stairs behind the stage, and arranged all my paraphernalia, and listed the times and signals from the wings: horns, trains, and whatever was needed in the plays. The simple party was fun.

Then the fun was over and the next day I saw my parents off at the station. So I was grown up at eighteen! Douglas sometimes took me for short drives in his car and taught me the rudiments of driving on the Clifton Downs. We talked about books and the things we liked, how Wilfred, pale and wide-eyed, a pathetic little boy, would have to go to school. I gathered his mother was a Russian actress; she was ill and asked Brownie to look after him, and that is how he arrived and was adopted. Douglas also landed on Brownie when he got installed with his printing press and opened shop, not long after he came down from Oxford. His parents were a sturdy Welsh couple, very proud of their son, but did not approve of his way of life. He went up to London for weekends, a lot, and — well, he had a good time.

Wye Valley — Tintern and Monmouth

Things were getting pretty grim, poverty was upon us and our depression was showing. Photographers were not getting orders as they used to. I was not experienced enough and I think my parents were wondering what to do with me. Brownie was very ahead of her time and the fees she charged for sittings were very high, but she was well known and very good. Just when I began to worry secretly Donald Hughes had a talk with me. He asked me whether I would like to go to his sister in Monmouthshire, who was starting up a community of various crafts and teachers. The Barn House was the basis of a reconditioned, or more like a rebuilt barn, big and spacious.

The farm dwellings around were being reconstructed and one could be made into a small studio and workroom for home photography. Already looms were set up and people were weaving cloth, rugs and scarves for sale down in Tintern. Pottery with one wheel to throw pots was being taught. The basics came first, finding and carting clays in, then washing and cleaning of the material in a long trough. The same applied to the wool that was washed, dyed and dried in the sun. Only organic dyes were used; where possible we collected plants ourselves. The ones which I delighted in were the outer onion skins which gave variable shades of orange and salmon-like tints, and walnut skins for deep rich browns.

Spinning in the open hall, near the looms, was an attractive scene. Margaret Hughes was a gifted woman with her German and Welsh languages. A Rudolf Steiner teacher, she attracted several young Germans who came over with their rucksacks and stayed a while. One, Margharetta, stayed six months. Some students learned the art of bread making and a balanced vegetarian cookery course. This was useful in supplying us with meals. They threw the clay on the wheel, made bowls and useful cottage ware. Then young miners who were sacked from the coal pits came up and were taught. All the work from the Brockweir Barnhouse was sold in Tintern, and eventually all the profits went to the men. A yearly display was held in the Westminster Central Hall. I went up with Margaret once, with a great stack of cloth, rugs, and pots; it was very demanding work. I suspect Donald Hughes did all the printing in Bristol and gave financial support. We did well.

In hindsight, I was very dilatory in not learning Welsh at school, and now in this border county of Monmouthshire it would have been useful.

A large area was being planted with blackcurrants, which were processed into the new drink "Ribena" now sold all over the world, containing a strong content of vitamin C, so nourishing for colds. Steep were the hills and cliffs that bordered the Wye River, with one main road on the Welsh side, the craft shop was on the road facing Tintern Abbey, its huge ruins were very exciting to wander around, noting the plants that had blown in. One could imagine ghosts were watching.

From Tintern, we walked up a rugged steep road to the top of the ravine to Brockweir, which only comprised a few cottages and a lane with dwellings below the Barn House. Here was "Downfield". We heard through Donald that James Floyd had bought the house and adjoining land — surprise, surprise. Nearby there was a house owned by Colonel and Mrs. Marriott whom I should meet later on and photograph.

While I was learning and absorbing all the new ideas I tried to feel at home in my stable-like studio but it was a tremendous change; electricity and water were available, but the Brownlee's Studio was very sophisticated for its time. I did not have transport and I had not the "feel" or knowledge of the locals. I knew I could miss out in photographic progress and everything was hard. But fate stepped in, gradually the old cough came back and I felt very lethargic. I felt better when James came up and sampled an evening meal; then he expected me down the lane on Sundays to Downfield. He had bought a horse for himself and a pony for me. But riding bareback on rough turf was a bit scary. I did three circuits all right and then the pony slightly shied and tore off. I don't remember falling but I woke up lying on a mattress in the hall of the Barn House. Margaret Hughes, James and a Miss Weaver were in attendance. I was groggy for two or three days. No one mentioned a doctor!

The season of the elvers returning home from the Atlantic up the Solway to the River Wye was an annual event; the long fine nets were spread across the river at certain places. Families were preparing to make the famous Wye Elevers Cheese bought by Fortnum and Mason and Harrods and probably, if enough, other firms. The elvers were taken in large containers to each house, which had large boiling coppers ready with large strainers. The baby eels were cooked in seconds, fished out, drained and pressed into cheeses. If you had not known what it was you wouldn't have guessed, there was no fishy or earthy taste. This delicacy was delicious and the Wye Valley inhabitants could ask the highest price. This small isolated industry only lasted 10-12 days. The bobbing lanterns, brilliant moonshine and excitement, make a thrilling event.

In June on Midsummer's Day we used to have a picnic, amidst a lovely ride (a wide unpaved road) which cut through a small forest; in olden days some parents and their children used to come up and gather wildflowers, and hopefully looked for fairies. Another country by-play was to visit the three witches on the edge of the Forest of Dean about 4.30p.m. in early autumn. The old women dressed in black had an open fire and a large cauldron. They brewed herbs and sometimes, I thought, blackberries in them. They chanted and sang verses in deep voices and gave out tea mugs of the brew. It was innocuous, but they entertained and presents were left. Their home was in the forest, but what a life. Two had black pointed hats, the real Welsh ones, the third a thick black shawl.

I began to sleep out of doors at night. It was thought the nightly fresh air would clear up my cough and chest. I had warm blankets and a black-coloured type of light tarpaulin. It was very cold in the morning when I came inside.

The Marriotts, who lived near James, began to ask us to Sunday roast lunch. I must say at the time I was very thin. I had not eaten any meat except at James' home. He admitted confidentially that he appreciated the cheeses and homemade bread, but was not smitten with the vegetarian dishes.

Colonel Marriott saw some of my photographs and wondered if I would photograph his wife. She would make an interesting study, but she was coloured and not supposed to be; James said it was one of those strange coincidences. Her parents who were a white English couple who lived in Jamaica, had this very English-featured dark child, the colour can come out four to five generations later.

The Marriotts were a devoted couple, and Mrs. Marriott did quite a bit of community work. James had a serious talk with me and said, "We are concerned about you and we have done something about it." Next day, a letter came to me from my parents and Margaret Hughes apparently had one. It was time I went home for a medical check and a home visit. Margaret was very civilised over it, I was not sure whether I was coming back or not but I packed up all my belongings and equipment. I went to the Radcliffe Hospital, Oxford, I think it was called the Infirmary in olden days, and had a thorough check-up. I had anaemia and a mild form of tuberculosis. Much later, I arrived in Monmouth itself, having been asked by the only photographer to come as an assistant. Work was scarce in all trades and professions.

The photographer was colourless, his studio bare with no flair, but he liked to take all the studio work himself. It was in the front part of an ordinary house, which he shared with an equally dull sister. I was to do the books, reception, help with printing and developing, and passports, which were scarce. This left the man to dash out and chase commercial work in Wales. I suggested throwing in presswork, which pays immediately. I alerted him about the Princess's Dolls' House which was to be driven from Wales to London. So off he went in hot pursuit; about 3p.m. one afternoon he phoned from a post office, "Get the darkroom ready I have got a scoop." Soon after he rushed in. The dolls' house had caught fire and he was the only photographer there.

I laid on the newspapers and an agent in London, and trains to take express packages. This I remembered from my training in Bristol, how speed was important for Brownie. We got three "exclusives" for the United States. The photographer had taken as many films as he could, the first puff of smoke, then flames until he was crowded out by police and firemen. Three days later the chap thanked me for my part. I got all the detail I could as we worked and I printed out paragraphs and captions for the prints. At least we caught the next day's London evening papers, and full reports with photographs in every daily paper the day after. I also took a phone call from New York which was a thrill.

I had rotten lodgings so I felt I must earn more. I called into a very nice homemade teas and dinner café, run by two elderly, charming Irish sisters. I asked them if they needed someone to do the washing up on a trial basis. Their place was packed out from 6p.m. to 10p.m. and the two ladies were very glad of the help.

When I had a few spare pounds I wandered over the narrow street into a repair garage run by a very decent man and his son; they usually had about 15 to 20 cars in for repairs and servicing. They said they hoped to have an Oxford Cowley in for sale. Meanwhile, one evening when I left the photographer after work, as I neared the garage, I saw smoke coming out of the main doors of the garage. I ran in and yelled out and the father clattered down some steps. A car was on fire in the garage, he pointed to me and to the cars whilst he attacked the flaming car. I was glad I had had lessons from Douglas and could reverse. I got out as many as I could, the street was so narrow and we had to leave space for the fire engine when it arrived; I was filthy. I limped into the café, and the sisters said, "We've put some clothes out in the bathroom upstairs." When I got downstairs, no one was ready for dinner. The fire was out in the garage; the men had lost or had several damaged cars. Next day they thanked me. The two ladies asked me if I would like the attic room to lodge in. They had given it some thought before, and I was amazed and delighted, nice furniture and pretty curtains.

When things had settled down, I managed to pay for the car. I drove over on a Sunday to the Barn House and parked it downwards facing the front door. Whilst we were drinking our tea, an awful crash! The handbrake had sprung off and I had left the gear in neutral. Fortunately there was only some scraping of the wooden lintel and the car was not badly dented.

James was away on one of his sketching treks, which could take weeks. In the 1920s he filled many sketchbooks with country scenes, making wide circuits. I was soon to return to Oxford and join my parents later for a while in Cornwall, where mother had bought a cottage with the money Granny Benson had left her. She had furnished it with simple things, and made the curtains, and let it for six months or more.

Whilst down there a photographic studio was up for sale or lease in St Ives; the owner was ageing and giving up. He was the only photographer in St. Ives. He seemed to do just bread-and-butter work, passports, weddings and some very staid and old-fashioned portraits. My father gave it a lot of thought and said an insurance policy was due to be cashed in and I could have that.

I was not making any headway with my job in Monmouth. St Ives was such a lovely place and there were great possibilities with the whole of West Penrith, the far west of Cornwall taking in Penzance, so negotiations proceeded. I could make shift and sleep in one of the workrooms. There was a decent bathroom and lavatory and basin. I could have the truckle fold-up bed we had at home and never used now.

Cornwall and St Ives — New Start, 1929–1933

At last my ideas and vision of what could be achieved in photography on a small scale were up to me. I had been left with an old but very good studio camera, the lens was good; the lighting and backdrops were dreadful and the paintwork disgraceful. A very serious young man called Cecil Coad was employed in the darkroom developing, printing and drying prints. He was very punctual, the eldest of a large family; his father was dead, so his work was very important to him. His loyalty to me was very vital, for him to accept change there would have been some anxiety at first.

I discussed some of my plans and relied on him to help me find the right-priced tradesmen. The studio was at the top of Tregenna Hill; it is very steep, and sometimes buses and tall vans nearly shaved us off the hill. Adjacent was the Catholic Church, right on the corner bend. I changed the shop front window to the bright Cornish blue so much used for yachts, being resistant to salt and wind. The shop window inside was a light brown wood, which I repainted a matt black. I felt this neutral background would offset anything we wished to display.

James Floyd later made a signboard: a large camera lens reflecting a beach scene and people. It was a striking oil painting slung in an ironwork frame that swung slightly. Three times in a month buses veered on to the narrow pavement but although knocked down, the sign was undamaged, so we gave up and propped it up in the shop.

The season to make money was obviously in the summer. Apart from the weather, one had to observe and take in the occupations of St Ives; the backbone of trade in the past was fishing. The herring season was very solid and organised through generations providing food, trade and auxiliary occupations like boat repairs, netting and painting. Pilchards were salted into barrels and exported. In June there was a short season of mackerel, a beautiful and well-flavoured fish — caught on lines with silver bait that flashed in the light. Sometimes people in the country were ill after eating it; that was because at the base of the tail was a small sac the size of a pea with a poison which should be cut out, only a few people were affected. In years to come smoked mackerel would be a delicacy. Roes were always kept and sold both soft and hard. (I have found that some countries throw these away.) From May to autumn there were regular visitors, then at the end of August we had in those days certain trade connections. I remember the first two weeks of August we had the Swindon trains, after them the itinerant Scottish fish-cleaners from Glasgow and even Aberdeen. Herring seasons were over in Scotland, the cold waters had come in.

Usually, photography had been taken for granted as just a method of recording events such as anniversaries, sports, weddings, crew postcards, and individuals, especially on holiday commercials, advertisements and so on. Photography as an art had not been totally accepted by the general public. So St Ives, Cornwall, was an inspiring place to work in. There was the St. Ives Artists' Colony, and across the peninsula the rival Newlyn Artists' Group. The wonderful scenery, the fishing boats and the colourful characters in the fishing fleets and the mining industry; history going back to the Phoenicians, the Spaniards, the Bretons and the Welsh who added their culture on to the original Cornish Celts, with the ancient Britons, all surrounded and steeped in the magnificent seascapes.

In the studio the lighting was perfected in the tight budget one has to impose upon oneself. We could begin the season with local new staff. Luckily people just came in like Hilda Guppy, a young woman who knew everyone, was good at figures and handling the shop. One burden, which was a necessity, was the film trade. We gave a 24-hour developing and printing service instead of the usual two days. Normally, films were sent away to a processing agent, so we did it ourselves and then eventually we had our simple blue covers instead of Kodak's colours. We sold Kodak, Ilford and later Agfa films.

Our supplies came from London and a few from Plymouth. The railway change at St Erth was always a stumbling block but if you lost the St Ives train you could easily meet up with it and the London train in 20 minutes by car. Transport was an essential ingredient, because I intended to launch into Press work with captions and/or up to two paragraphs for added value. Eventually, I employed a man who had done a lot of commercial and outside work and as a bonus had his flying license. He brought his motorbike. His family lived near London.

I could concentrate on "At home photography of pets and children". I also tried to attract visitors from the larger hotels by being available for portraits in the studio in the evenings after their dinner. Coffee was on hand and sherry in small glasses. Whilst I was adjusting the huge unwieldy camera, we talked and I listened to what they had seen and explored, and I tried to keep up to date with future local events that might be interesting. I only took one family or couple each night because I developed the films immediately and needed time. They were dried and ready for Cecil to print proofs in the morning. We needed another boy to deliver and run errands and clean periodically during the day in the workroom. It was very important to clear dust and print trimmings away. Some shopkeepers in the town were regular customers. We saw that the work was delivered to them on time, or before. Our Press work was steadily increasing, fitting in with sporting groups and weddings. The latter I avoided and let Mr. Butt do.

We did a good line in postcards. Our coup was the outdoor Shakespeare theatre on the south coast at Porthcurnow. The sea was a stunning background to the three or four plays running through the two weeks every evening, except Sundays. I was up all night, and had to sleep when I could after printing batches of a thousand cards. They sold out the seats so we just sold out our cards accordingly.

I had made friends with many artists including Bernard Leach, the great potter known all over the world. He allowed me to exhibit one or two large pieces of his wonderful work. I liked to dress the window every week. For portraits, if they were customers I always asked permission to display them; but not my models, because I could use them for the future. I visited Mr. Drage, the owner and manager of our local cinema, and suggested that instead of the ancient advertisements we could brighten up the scene with a local model from a new shop or a trade. I paid for my own advertisement and used a new local photograph, changing it within the rules of the cinema as often as I could.

I cannot remember the exact circumstances when I met Algernon Blackwood in St Ives. He had a deeply lined face and a magical voice. He was staying in St Ives and we got into conversation, I would have told him that his book *The Education of Uncle Paul*, and other stories he had written, fascinated me. I asked him if I could take his photograph, which I did. Because of his ghost stories he was called "The Ghost Man". I selected some prints and sent them to London where he lived. I have his charming letter of thanks. As I had the copyright, I hoped they would be used because he is unlike anyone I had ever met. He travelled a great deal especially to Canada and the States; he was a riveting storyteller.

A newcomer arrived from up country with her hats and accessories; the lady was photogenic, and at the same time became a new customer for the cinema advertisements, and also the Chamber of Commerce. I was very touched to be asked to be on the Council of the Chamber of Commerce, it gave me an insight into expanding trades. In the winter we had to rely on shipwrecks for the Press, and stock up with new views and winter sports. Things were pretty tight for everyone between January and March. I used to help out at the Copper Kettle Café for evening meals, and was given a meal in return. I managed to get a few evenings in May when the early strawberries came in.

Weaving in and out I made some wonderful friends. I had introductions, which helped. The Lindner family almost "adopted" me. Hope Lindner, the daughter, was very gifted and lived in London; she had her own life, and confessed she felt guilty for not living with her aged parents. She bequeathed me her garage. Her mother was a dear, gentle personality; she loved her walled garden, I called her Aunt Gussie. Uncle Moffat was an original founder of St Ives Artists' Society. I usually had Sunday lunch with them and, when I could, dropped in for coffee after dinner.

When Hope arrived on her rare visits we were surrounded by the various young twenties who had reappeared to visit their parents. Sometimes our jollifications filled me with horror, but we were never too much beyond the pale, even when a Royal Navy frigate put in for a visit. All I remember is one young officer landed in our shop window during a shore party, and became a shop dummy activated by a charade we made up, much to the amusement of a passing crowd. My camera was very busy at that time. Looking back, we were not involved in any drinking spree, just high spirits. While my uptown friends' parents were busy giving hospitality, downtown fishermen were proudly showing their new friends their fishing gear, and of course the local pub on the wharf "The Sloop".

When the Navy left, we were very busy with the full season of tourists; day-trippers were not actual customers except for the odd film or two. We turned to aviation photography — the plan was to sketch out all the possibilities which had never been done before.

Gerald Butt knew the Surrey Aviation Club which hired out airplanes. We worked out the cost of a pilot to bring a plane to St Ives, with Butt to fly it for four days.

The plan I envisaged worked well for the weather forecast. The District Council was putting in main drainage across to the Penzance area which was full of historic pre-Celtic areas. A veritable treasure-trove for land mapping by air, if one got the finest films and experimental infra-red material. This land survey by air would save hours for the authorities.

Next on the list were the large hotels — taken close up and swooping shots over tennis courts with hotel guests on a fixed afternoon playing. A sure customer was the Golf Links with players on the greens and the sea backdrop for a new brochure. In between we fitted in postcard view shots of St Ives and Penzance and rugged parts of the Peninsula.

It was a successful time, interviewing the architects, surveyors, and engineers in the Council offices. I drew up a simple contract which satisfied all our customers. Proofs were given after a deposit of £50 at the signing of the contract. The deposits paid for the airplane hire.

Gerald Butt built a wooden frame to be screwed on the body structure to hold my heavy Adams camera rigid. I was to sit behind Butt, the pilot. We learned signals to suit our work; light airplanes were open to the elements in those days. I had telephoned both Kodak and Ilford about what we wanted to do. Ilford I found to be more generous and experimental over films.

I fished out my riding breeches and jacket and wore a brimmed Heath felt hat. We worked out every detail: timing, weather and aircraft care. That was the luckiest and most rewarding time. Our customers were delighted. Earlier, we had rented an old cellar near the back beach by the artists' studios. It had water laid on and we converted it into another dark room for the commercial side.

I was lucky to be able to leave Hilda to deal with all our expenses. I always did the banking, especially in the winter when money was pretty short. That was when I really got thin. The Bank was very patient and sometimes scolding.

At Christmas 1932, I decided to close the studio for two weeks from 1 January. On Boxing Day at 11a.m.

Dr. Woodward telephoned from Combe, Oxford, that my father had died suddenly at 10a.m. I said I would leave in one hour. I rang Aunt Gussie and told her that I would be driving up and taking the car. I was quite calm, knowing I had a long, long drive of just less than 300 miles in the bright blue, friendly, two-seater Oxford Cowley. I kept her topped up and ready for action like the pony I used to ride. I always found time to check her over weekly. Such a simple mechanical task in those days.

Aunt Gussie quietly said, "I am very sorry, it will be a difficult time." She had asked the cook to make me a good array of food, plus a thermos. I was very touched. Goodbye St Ives, my freedom now will end. Arrangements would be made to look after my mother in St Ives with her possessions. I had no idea when or how, but something would turn up. I was not religious but I tried to return my thanks in my own way by action because I never had much money. I suppose I gambled with life by ideas and visions, I suppose I have been naive even to this day.

I drove out of the back lane up to the hill overlooking the bay and past Tregenna, to Hayle and on to the road that would take me east until I eventually got to Oxford. It was a cold, dry day. I was well wrapped up as there was no heating in cars in those days. I knew my route well. Bodmin moor would be wonderful, a pity I could not stop and take some shots. I planned to stop near Jamaica Inn and have my sandwiches or whatever had been carefully packed up. So, alone, I carefully thought out alternatives for my mother. My Uncle

George was our solicitor and he would take care of the legal side. I would have to find accommodation in St Ives for my mother. The tailor next door had vacated the flat over his shop and moved to a house. I hoped he would consent to my renting his place. There were two spacious rooms and a bedroom and very small kitchen, a little balcony enough to take two chairs and a stool, overlooking the bay like I had already got extending from our workrooms. I could knock part of the wall down, and put a door in and make quite a decent place. Mother would have to sell our baby grand piano, anyway no one played on it now; it had a lovely tone. Past teatime, another stop. Eventually I got to Combe at midnight; all the village lights were on in the houses. I drove to the back gate and parked the car.

People were moving in and out of the house — my mother was ill. Someone took the keys from me and removed the suitcase and bits and pieces. I thanked everyone; the Salvation Army were there. I had a bath, went down to my father's study and drew up a list for the next day. I found my father's notebook. I was told Uncle George was arriving in the morning with the undertaker. I then fell asleep in my own room and woke up early feeling very alone. I always felt guilty that father had to work with only one eye fully functional throughout the Christmas services until he died, with no retirement. Now it was up to me to care for my mother. I can only thank the staunchly kind people of the parish and my Aunt and Uncle who saw us through.

At dawn I was visited by the Salvation Army who asked me what clothes I had got for the funeral — I looked at them blankly until the senior good lady offered to take me to Oxford, to get a suitable coloured coat. I thought, yes I'll go if I can go to Lincoln College and I could get some advice and liaise with the Bishop. So I bought a fine check black and white coat and a small black hat. I wrote out the death notices in the local paper office with copies to the other papers. The Rector of Lincoln College arranged the date of the funeral with the Bishop. We then raced back to Combe in time to be with my Uncle and Aunt. That night I told the Churchwardens I would take one place in the church to guard the coffin every three or four hours with them from dusk to dawn; the tall wooden candlesticks at each corner with large flames. This was the night before the funeral. My mother was still in bed, I popped in and out but she was shocked.

I had no idea who anybody was at first; the church was packed. The aunts were unknown to me as they had arrived and stayed in Oxford. I met them all in the dining room, where we had catered for enough. The two Bishops spoke highly of father, and how hard he had worked for the bells' installation; they left early. The contents of the house, including the lovely dining table with extra leaves, were auctioned in Oxford and went for a song.

I returned to Cornwall ahead of mother's arrival and arranged accommodation in the empty flat next door over the tailor's shop, which was quite roomy with reasonable facilities. I got curtains made and hoped mother would not miss her garden too much. St Agnes Cottage was long-leased to a couple of Australians from Sydney, so she could not go there.

Mother had quite a few friends in Cornwall. I was able to drive her over to see them and they would drive her back. Then two old friends of hers bought a house quite near for their retirement. The Church of England in those days had no pension fund for clergy, so the little money left by my father was very small.

I began a fresh year of business which was very slack until March — a hard time for all. One had to order stock for the season and not run out; the banks got fidgety and one desperately chased up accounts due by lagging customers. Shipwrecks and lifeboat activities were rewarding in the way of news, and the occasional fire was newsworthy.

Later my mother moved into a cottage belonging to a farm, which was on a bus route from St Ives. She had access to a paper delivery via the bus. The farm had eggs, milk, butter and cream and occasional meat: poultry and pork. She had made the two-bedroom cottage very attractive with its grey stonewalls. A small garden front and back, and a solid stone "hedge" around to keep animals out. The farm also cropped cauliflowers and cabbages, which went out on to the Cornish night trains to London. She could take a "head" whenever she wished. I would pop up when I could with fish and groceries and postage stamps. Down to the cliffs, the view was spectacular.

One person I admired and sometimes met and walked with was the great pianist Paderewski, a small man with a shock of white hair. He was very frail. He came down to St Ives and had a flat for a few weeks with a housekeeper. He said little but was a kindly soul.

Prior to the move I changed my Oxford Cowley to a conventional, square, saloon car — looking at it in a photograph it was grotesquely ugly. I cannot remember where or when I got it, but for a while I stayed with a friend who had two lively small girls — I often photographed them and when I could we'd go for picnics — thus, I suppose was the need for a bigger car, also it was useful in moving goods and furniture. Gradually, I was feeling very tired and depressed, also my friends were going away for work. Hope got married and told us all afterwards! In fact I was near a breakdown: my bank manager who had been wonderfully kind advised me to sell the studio whilst I could; my operator was helping the local chemist, wanted my business and would buy it and he would run it. I had a lot of trouble over the second darkroom which was being misused.

An Interval to Stranger Things

I cannot remember going to a doctor but I had stretched myself and knew I had had it. My friend and two children had decided to go to Hampshire to Petersfield, which she knew well and was near a suitable school. My mother had found and made quite a lot of friends, she had a glorious view of the sea. Father Delaney was very kind to me at this time. I took my friend and her family to St Erth, where they caught the London train and would stay with their grandfather, W.W. Jacobs, the author of many tales of the docks and ships in London. He and I were great friends; I found his dry humour memorable. In fact all that family were literary.

My great wrench was leaving Aunt Gussie and Uncle Moffat, also Bernard Leach and his sessions with his pupils who stayed at the Pottery. Mother did not approve of my going to Petersfield but I told her that it was very temporary, in fact it was for about two or three weeks. I went to a very good woman doctor, who said I needed rest and regular meals. She said, "Here is an introduction to a mother and daughter who have a home. They are dedicated to restoring professional people to work." She smiled and said, "I hope you like classical music!" So I went to Mrs. Dore and her daughter Clare, up a rambling lane off a tarmac road which led to two big gates. The large house on the front left had a wonderful garden. Another house facing the other way had a weedy drive, which led down to a large brick house and overgrown tennis lawn. I drove slowly up to that front door and rang the bell.

Thus I met Clare Dore. She was slight and very lame from polio, with dancing dark brown eyes and a lovely smile. She gave me a great welcome. The rooms were large and the main room was a comfortable music-room with a grand piano — a couple of music stands on the side, comfortable chairs, Persian rugs, lovely polished furniture and large windows.

It was explained that it was a home in the real sense; her mother and she had been living in Durban and so many friends had come to England who begged them to come over, so they did. They found they could be useful in helping overtired workers. Kitty Ormerod was the instigator. I was not to worry about money, if I could drive them occasionally for shopping and to the station to meet guests who were usually teachers, doctors or musicians. I was assured it was usually one visitor at a time. They had light musical nights over the weekend but at first I was to rest, read and get well. So that was my first breakdown with a happy start.

My first two days I had breakfast in bed and asked if I might wander round the garden and assess the possibilities. Apparently before the Dores bought the house it had been empty for a while; when occupied there was a full-time gardener and staff. A very nice person called Lucy, living only a quarter of a mile down the road and married, had her mother living with them who saw Lucy's two children off to school, so that Lucy could go to work for the Dores.

Apparently, Dr. Ormorod used to drop in for a cup of tea about twice a week, and sometimes for a Sunday early musical evening. Every weekend Helius arrived from London with her violin (she taught music somewhere in London). She also came from Durban but her grandparents and an aunt came from Appledore in the North.

I wandered around the place and decided that the drive had a good foundation, but had a lot of moss and small grasses, which could easily be dealt with. Over one hedge I sensed there was a good-sized kitchen garden. I gasped a bit at first as it was just choked up. The soil was excellent underneath. A big fork and a hoe and perhaps a mattock could knock it over. The tennis court was sunk down, with a steep bank with steps from the house. The grass had been cut now and then. The shrubbery around had some good trees and rhododendrons and flowering shrubs.

I then decided I would clean up the car — I had some money left over in the bank — just capital. I would have doctor's bills eventually and I ought to pay for my keep. I found Clare and her mother, who was quite tall and of a biggish build. I found it was difficult to approach them on the matter of money. Mrs. Dore smiled and excused herself. Clare said it was their work and pleasure to restore people to health or to give them a pause from exhausting work. "If we use your car we will pay for petrol but we do not want any money from you, but if and when you are rested perhaps some ideas for the garden — nothing heavy at the moment though. Kitty Ormorod will be here this afternoon and tell you what you must avoid." So I looked at her and said, "It's my chest isn't it?" She nodded, "I think you've been through a lot." I then said, "Well, it might be a good idea to start a salad and herb patch in the kitchen garden; it is so protected away from trees and has full sunlight."

The Sunday evenings were delightful, just Clare, Helius and a guest/friend would discuss what they would play — one piece led to another. Someone would start playing, the others then orchestrated in. We stopped for an evening meal.

In the end it was several weeks before I left. I was delayed by having to go to Haslemere to the nearest dentist. He was very good but I had to have a wisdom tooth out, my first-ever extraction. My teeth are like rocks and this one was firmly embedded with roots running beneath adjacent teeth. It took two hours to get it out and several injections. The sweat was pouring down the poor man's face. I felt dreadful and was sorry for him. It took me a bit of time to leave, two hours in fact. I crossed the road to where the car was parked and I remember starting the engine, then felt myself falling and quickly turned the petrol off. I woke up in a restaurant empty except for two men — a policeman and a man with a white apron exclaiming, "She is round." When I managed to get up the policeman took me solicitously to the car. I don't know how I got to Liss but I did. Clare was horrified, got me to bed and Kitty Ormorod had my face put in a splint. My jaw was broken; that meant six weeks. The pain was sometimes unbearable.

I looked forward to my raw egg beaten up with sherry every evening before my soup or custard which I sucked in, not through a straw, but a sort of jug mug with a long spout with which one sucked up soft foods.

Anyway, I was not idle when I got my mind adjusted to dressing and getting on with a light gardening method. But I did not make much impression. I was reminded to write to my mother — I felt that I wanted to detach myself from everyone I knew. I did ring up and enquire about the two small girls of my past friend down the road at Petersfield. They actually said they missed me, which was surprising.

I began to feel very much better, so I began to scan newspapers for work of any sort to get into earning a living again. During this time I heard that James Floyd had moved to Cuckfield, Sussex. I went to Cuckfield to visit and whilst there I enjoyed all the planting round the lake and a new studio near his house. He had been making trips on his bicycle to different counties sketching. From his sketchbooks he then did oils or large watercolours. Then I happened to hear about a woman driver needed for delivering homemade cakes and bread; I presented myself and got the job, with some misgivings. This was at Hayward's Heath. I felt I had James behind me — I was determined to work my way out of a hopeless bog with no definite future.

Sussex — Haywards Heath

Advertisement:
Wanted — A lady van driver for local round
of homemade bread and cakes.

I saw it in the window of a very high quality homemade bread and cake shop, specialising in weddings and anniversaries. The restaurant was open for lunches, teas and dinners, except on Sundays. The cake shop was part of the eating area but had another entrance to the street and one at the back to the kitchen. There were four women cooks and I, also in the kitchen, because I had to be there from 5.30a.m. to 6a.m. to lift the loaves out of the two large built-in ovens, tap all the loaves and put them on trays. Then two or three of us had breakfast, a good one: eggs and bacon, toast, etc. Two women were going on with batches of scones. I loaded up the van with orders of cakes, then the bread and lastly scones, just out of the oven.

The van was awful; it was shaped like a great big loaf with the restaurant's name on it. I never knew why the last driver left, nor the ones before that. No one liked the owners, Major and Mrs. Young — very, very army. He spoke to us just within politeness range, very correctly with surnames. Apparently the round had been run down, there were just the regular people and no new customers. Gradually, the pace accelerated so that I had to divide my visiting on certain days for my new people. I was allowed to take a full long tray of extras; often I was introduced from another customer. I made some delightful friends. The Major actually called it initiative when I came back by 4p.m. sold out.

We had a very competent person called Quinn who had seen better times, but she had the touch for doing complicated cake decorations. She suddenly began relying on me for quantities, so in the right-hand deep pocket of my white coat I kept a packet of cards on which I put the recipes down. I always left them in the kitchen end, where we hung our overalls. One awful day I had a short round, the day I used to scrub all the trays out, check my boxes and bags, etc. I walked into the kitchen and Quinn called out, "Daphne, check me on my Viennese, for six (cakes)." I slipped my overall on as I saw the Major going down the benches. I was quietly guiding Quinn, card in hand and multiplying the amounts. The Major with great fury yelled at me. By then I was certain he must have been a pseudo-Sergeant-Major, not an officer or a gentleman. "How dare you steal our recipes?" I was stunned. Furiously, I said that I was not a thief. He accused me of divulging his secret, copyright recipes and dismissed me on the spot. He ordered me to hand over my pack of cards. Quinn was quietly weeping; I knew she had a memory problem, not a cooking one.

I told him how hard everyone worked and when the kitchen was overloaded I only helped out with quantities by request, to speed things up. I saw a cheerful fat cook turn round and wink at me. She was a tower of strength physically and addressed the Major as if nothing had happened. "The cards have been a wonderful help, Major, I am sure Daphne has never made a cake in her life; anyway it's time we had our break." She came over and said, "Come on to the caff", and ignored the man. Overalls were hung up and we asked the waitress for our tea break. I said to my friend in need (I'll call her Rosie), "*You* are not scared of the Major, are you?" "No," she said, "I could get a job anywhere, because he knows I've made bread all my life. I am strong and it suits me at the moment." We talked about Quinn. I took Rosie's advice and went on working.

I think I spent the Saturday evening and Sunday with my friend James to discuss the future; he was only a short bus trip away. I said, "I'll be moving on when I can get another job. I will tell my couple where I lodge, it's important they know." James sucked his pipe, said nothing. He then said, "I've liked the bread and cakes." As staff, if anything was left we could pay for it at half price. Sunday night I came back early and sat in the kitchen with the nice couple where I lodged. The husband always knocked on my door and checked me out with a cup of tea in the morning. He was a railway tracklayer and tapped the rails, beginning at 5a.m.

between the trains. We lived in the railway cottages with neat gardens; they were especially built for workers and belonged to the railway. Bathing was in the laundry with a boiler and a dipper. I told them that as soon as I found something I would give them warning.

I then answered my next advertisement and I felt I might get the job. Time to move on, my own customers were very sad and some wanted to write to me when I said I was leaving. I was stronger now.

Petworth, Sussex

I answered an advertisement for a photographic assistant to cover outdoor events for a photographer who was established and worked for a Sussex paper, also doing local work, but they wanted "colour" by paragraphs or minor feature articles. I had sold my car, which was not worth much but I could give my wonderful friends the Dores at Liss a decent present. For my new job a motorbike was provided for work. I arrived at Petworth by two buses — actually Liss was not so far away. The formal bus stop was near the butcher's shop, so I went in and asked the butcher where I could get lodgings. I had two suitcases and my cameras. He told me I could leave my things at his place whilst I went to the photographer.

I went up the road to the new man. A new studio was at the end of a detached longish house with plenty of land around it. It had two entrances — one for the private dwelling, the other for business. I was received by a very nice woman, who was tall and welcoming, but in her eyes was a calculating look — I felt perhaps I was not up to her hopes. Her husband then came through, a thin, small, busy little man, polite but I was not impressed at all. In fact I was disappointed. I was to start at 9a.m. unless there were press appointments afar. I had to calculate bad weather with the bike. I asked about it, it was not a make I knew so I tried it and asked about purchasing fuel. There was a good back-rack which helped.

They expected me to find my own lodgings, so I returned to the butcher. His wife said if her daughter's room would suit, I could have that as she was married and gone away. They would provide breakfast and every meal if I shared it with them in the large warm kitchen. That suited me well. The bathroom was on the ground floor with a generous water supply.

The next part was a catalyst or the arrow on target to connect me with Kent and the war.

So I had lodgings with the Family Butcher of Petworth. They showed me unsurpassed kindness after I left the photographer, which was difficult because he was a weasel of a man who always had a yellow muffler, never parted with it. He was flatly boring to work with.

I went out on assignments to incidents, weddings, and local events. One afternoon I returned to the studio and my employer wanted my films developed at once, as he had started with the film tanks. My St Ives dark room had a system which I copied from my training days. When work was in progress we had a red light outside the door which we turned on when developing began, so any messages were spoken loudly, starting with, "Can you talk?" After about 10 minutes' work, whilst waiting for the "fixing" period, the Weasel grabbed me, made me turn around and made a pass. One look at him and I gave him a hard slap, shut the door on him and walked through to his Missus, and said, "I'm sorry to say, I have to give my notice in. Your husband made advances", or something similar. "I don't want any money. Thank you for being kind to me whilst I've been here." I remember her saying, "I've had trouble before."

I walked back down the road, it was about 3.00p.m. My startled landlord said behind the counter of piled-up meat, "What's this, coming in this time of day?" I said, "I've left my job. Given my notice in."

He left the counter and we went through to a large kitchen. He called out "Mother, can you come down?" I cannot tell you how kind and thoughtful they were. Father got *The Times* newspaper in the early morning; he got the job pages for me to find work and he helped by not charging me for telegrams and stamps and all my meals as I waited. So that is how I landed in Kent as a manager of Ditton Court Farm Shop on the London to Folkestone Road.

Ditton Court Farm, Kent — County of Produce

Mr. Bennet gave me an interview and lunch after I was met at the station. Benny told me afterwards that the reasons he gave me the job were that I was so pathetically thin; my prompt answers by telegram and appointment (he thought the initiative was there); my knowledge of French; my interest in the pedigree Jersey herd; my liking of his well bred pigs; my knowledge of vegetables, and readiness to start work. He put me back on the train and said he had others to see and he would let me know. After changing trains and buses, I reached Petworth that evening, and "Mother", the two sons and my saviour butcher cheered and said "You've got the job. Mr. Bennet has just telephoned and will confirm it to you. Tomorrow you'd like to go shopping I expect. Here's something to go on with," and handed me an envelope. Later I managed to repay my fares and sent them a present.

88

If I had not gone to Kent I might not have got into the RAF or met all the wonderful friends I have had and still have in Australia.

When I arrived at Ditton Court Farm, I was taken down to the London Road, opposite the Farm shop where I would be living. Mrs. Smith was a very elderly grandmother who gave me a great welcome. She had lived alone for some time but her son and daughter-in-law lived very near. To my delight she was French of pure Huguenot descent. She was very proud of her small but packed vegetable garden and her cooking, on which I was to thrive. Next day, I was to go to Maidstone to be fitted for suitable clothes for the shop. In the winter it would be very cold. The long Canadian log building was well built but the front had tall shutters that slid round each side and were heavily barred inside. A long mahogany polished counter and shelves behind had come from a ship. The counter was very wide and contained all the accoutrements needed underneath. On top were scales, baskets and jars of honey and homemade jams. The wooden walls were rather bare but I was to build up trade with all the farm produce, and as specials the odd crops which could not be sent to markets.

I was given *carte blanche* in what I bought in, provided it was fresh and excellent quantity. This I enjoyed very much and I was handed on from one producer to another; a lot of ex-service people were running poultry, keeping bees and unusual produce. We did not run to flowers or plants, which could be very costly for main-road custom and weather.

My routine was to walk a fair step up to the farm to the Steward's office by 6a.m., in attendance was the Farm manager and the Owner, Mr. Bennet. We sat at a long table and the Steward had got the early morning market price for barley, wheat, fruit and vegetables, and later hops. There were 500 acres of vines; a herd of pure Jerseys, about 30 plus; bacon pigs — 200 blacks and 300 whites. Actually, the large whites were the ace: their configuration had to be bred and fed to perfection; the bacon feed was measured and the mix was to keep the animals in perfect shape without any surplus fat. The Blacks were of excellent flavour for pork, but black bristles on the rind were not attractive on bacon. The sties were spotless. Straw was frequently changed and the front pens had excellent drainage. When well housed the pig is very exacting. Their feed was always kept away from their excrement, which they controlled. I was taught a great deal and learned to respect and avoid the boars.

Our main crops were hops, barley, apples, pears, cherries, plums, raspberries, strawberries, gooseberries, currants, potatoes, beetroot for canning (size 10 to a large can), cabbages, cauliflowers, and sometimes peas. The pickers were locals from Larkfield village and were, of course, seasonal.

East Malling Research Station had acquired part of the estate and used our material for research, which was perfecting produce for the canning industry, improving on new techniques, and watching the effects of using new varieties. Size, taste, and flavour were the combined features.

The staff was not constant in the past and it was up to me to rectify that. There seemed no shortage of applicants but I was to make sure I had an honest and knowledgeable right hand. I was lucky in my Mrs. Smith, who never mixed much with Larkfield; her family, not many yards away, were in Aylesford, where the large paper mills were. A tall young woman rang me and asked if I might see her. She was just what we wanted. She was experienced in shop-keeping, good at figures and had excellent references. We had a young lass part-time called Lily, she was honest and cheerful and was glad to work full time. We were open seven days a week in the full fruit season.

By Easter, we began to sell dressed chickens by order. We were offered good-quality birds but no one would sell them ready to cook. As I had got the demand I risked it. With Mrs. Beaton's cook book and much urging on by Mrs. Smith I dressed quite a few with distaste, but they sold well.

The housekeeper plus family friend offered to do a good line in fudge; eventually we had five flavours, also excellent coconut ice. We had two large blackboards on which we put our new things and specials up. The juicy Czar plums (excellent for jam and as a dessert) I remember in large round baskets, 7 lbs for 2/-.

Fred the driver brought the Bedford round to the loading bay at the back and unloaded potatoes in their sacks in a storeroom. There were several kinds: we used to advise our customers which were good for baking, for roasting and chips, and how to keep them white either with vinegar or milk in boiling. All were displayed with their names. I told Benny I expected free potatoes, as I was always experimenting in Mrs. Smith's kitchen.

One lunchtime I glanced at Granny Smith's daily paper — headlines of the disappearance of a young Oxford sculptor. When I was at school, Hester Munro used to stay with us in the summer. After Christmas I used to join the Munro family at Lincoln College, Oxford.

Mrs. Munro and Helen, Hester's sister, decided to have some time in Innsbruck, a favourite retreat of theirs. They travelled there and arrived at a hotel at the end of the township near the mountains. About 3p.m. Mrs. Munro said she would unpack and rest in her room, whilst Helen said she would walk up the mountain road and would be back for tea just after 4p.m. She never returned. By 6p.m., I think, the hotel began a small search party and then the police took over. There was no sign. After four days someone went way off the track and noticed something he thought out of place; he went through scrub and round boulders into a cave of horror. Helen was bound and gagged, raped and naked, she must have only just died. A fire had been burning and there was evidence of occupation. By this time the news had spread and a countrywoman of many miles away went to the police, in fear. She told them of her horror of her husband's cruelty — he used to go off for weeks and return in a horrible state. She had children and she sought police protection from him. She said he had not returned yet, but was due. The man walked straight into the police trap. He was sentenced for life and every year on the dreadful day he was flogged.

Mrs. Smith gallantly brought over my lunch tray to the office so one or both helpers could go home. Sometimes Benny came down in his bright yellow Bentley, a big open type, and watched with his beady eyes. He would climb out eventually and have a look at the crops growing up to the fences either side of the shop.

We now had regular London customers who gave orders for their return sometimes daily or at regular intervals. Meanwhile Europe was beginning to feel the anti-Jewish turmoil simmering from Germany. Many Jews with relatives here entered Britain. The population on the whole did not take Hitler seriously. I was alerted by a strange paradox. One customer, was Mary S. Allen, the pioneer policewoman, also defender of women's rights. The issue was very complicated. Mary Allen had uncovered a network of slave traffic in England and Europe. Other women were forming many movements, which caused confusion and misunderstanding. I was given quite a lot of literature about what was being done; it seemed to be essential to overcome the ambitions between Germany, Russia, Fascism and the Jewish race. Whatever the outcome, women had to be trained into a helpful force to combat conflict of the future.

I had no money or influence. I knew Benny's definite opinions in breeding a healthy race, whether it was humans or his agricultural stock, cows, pigs and fruit stock, "Destroy the runts, breed for quality", and so on.

I suggested the idea of gathering a small nucleus of some of our customers without ties, young women with cars and with time to spare. The list offered to the young women workers would be to:

1. attend St John's ambulance classes in first aid, and later Air Raid Warden training;
2. learn to drive a vehicle up to Ambulance Standard;
3. mobilise and join into a Women's Auxiliary Group later.

Our target was mainly factory workers and shop assistants. I approached the director of Aylesford Paper Mills, Colonel Sheldon, a charming man, widowed and living in a house nearby. His contribution was, when I was ready, to go to the factory and address the girls themselves. He would make time available, by changing the evening times with time off for classes and so on. He asked me to tell them the role of women needed in war. He had of course been through the role of Aylesford Paper Mills if there was to be a war.

There was a start at once, with five or six women ready to teach so many a week. Classes were already filling up rapidly for First Aid. Then we were offered by industry to be taught flying for £12.10.0 fee at Ramsgate at weekends, spending Saturday evening under canvas.

I spoke to Benny, but he had his scouts out already to see what I was up to. He did not approve, yet he agreed about the flying. I was being very careful, because he was a very clever businessman and a complete mystery. He had been a merchant in dried fruit and exotic foods in the Middle East. He had been to Bonn University and spoke several languages; his general knowledge was inexhaustible. He was a very large man, now ageing and putting on a lot of weight.

For my first real holiday I had to ask Benny to consider back holiday pay, because I was taking my mother to France for three and a half weeks. He was surprised when I told him that the French Government Tourist Office had given the different itineraries, and I had mapped out one to cover the Roman era. I would delay my talk to the mill workers until I returned. I was watching European politics closely, and I felt time was very short. The French system for travelling then was very neat; the ticket application was a sheet of paper with France's railway system, and you traced your route without returning on your tracks. You could stop for as long as you wanted, and catch buses or trains extra if they branched out to short stops. My mother and I set off directly to Paris within one week. We met local friends, the Vitrys, there, then headed for Lyons, stopping and having bed and breakfast all the way to Sête, Perpignan, Carcassonne and returned through the west to Paris and back to Kent. I am glad my mother had a wonderful time. We returned with photographs of places which later were destroyed.

Upon my return, I put my mother on the Penzance train after she stayed overnight in Kent. She looked so well. She enjoyed the parts of France she had never been to, all the old Roman buildings, the country meals in small wayside hotels; the weather was very good to us. I felt the unease, and even suspicion and fear amongst the French. In Paris, soldiers were much in evidence. The England I had returned to was hopelessly asleep. The day I went down to the Mill, and addressed the women for the 4.30p.m. gathering, their hall was packed.

I met Colonel Sheldon and a couple of senior staff. I had not prepared the talk. I know I began with the words, "This early morning Czecho-Slovakia was invaded by the Germans and as we gather here the country is now partly occupied; this is the beginning of Hitler's domination of Europe." I explained that our country needed trained women in many ways. I referred them to the various services and existing women's corps but training in First Aid, and learning to drive with five women owner-drivers, were available in Larkfield, and other useful courses were to be considered. I left the rest to the Colonel, because the Mill would be preserved for the war effort.

I began my drill and regulations in the Maidstone Barracks of the 19th Royal West Kents. We were offered the choice — Army or Royal Air Force. The Royal Navy had not yet formulated a women's section.

My talk to women was reported fully in the local press and one London newspaper. My boss Benny was furious. Commandant Mary Allen was angry and surprised. I was upset about the latter, and very puzzled. Then I realised she had been, and was, a friend of Hitler; she was also a friend of the Mitfords — what a mess. I worked stolidly on, and then Benny came down with three men by the side of the shop, Army; I walked up to them and I guessed why. They were measuring out a great bed of ripening Royal Sovereign strawberries; in a week they would be ripe. Benny coldly looked at me and said, "This is to be a gun site and they will start work this week." To see this good crop vandalised was just the beginning to what the land was going to look like.

Although plants that man had planted were pulled up and brutalised, I still felt sad about these ways of doing things, but it was war and that is the way it happens. I then talked to Granny Smith, saying I would soon have to get another job before I was called up — things would get more and more difficult. The early apples were being picked; the best were going to market. I often went with Fred, the lorry driver, for the 4a.m. Tuesday market at the Borough. Volunteers were signing up; I had breakfast in the Market pub after unloading. Normally I never did, but I shook hands with Fred's mates and we wished each other good luck. Going back Fred said, "So this is it then?" I said, "I'm seeing the boss tonight," which I did. As I always had dinner with the family on Wednesdays, I thought I had better give my notice in before. But Benny said to come to dinner and say goodbye then, "I will miss you, but you are doing the wrong thing."

I had answered an advertisement requiring a woman chauffeur in Buckinghamshire for which I was accepted. I began a new life, temporarily of course, near Chalford St Giles, at the Chatford Manor Hotel. I had an interview in London in St James with a very wealthy woman who was part-owner of a famous firm, importing and distributing luxury foods. I was surprised that I was considered. I honestly told her that I had given up my job, and would be called up if and when war was declared. Apart from keeping the car clean and in running order, I was no mechanic, and she affirmed that was done by the Rover agent. I said I could start over the weekend. I was to be a companion as well as driver and have my meals with her. She had a large suite in the hotel. She asked what needlework I did and I shook my head, no knitting, and no tapestry. "Oh dear," she said very bleakly, "what on earth do you do in the evenings?" I said I read a lot, she brightened up at that. "Well you will have to amuse me!"

I arrived at Gerrard's Cross Station and was met by a hotel car. The hotel itself was very spacious in a lovely park. There was no swimming pool, but there were eleven male chauffeurs; our cars were in a neat row of garages which must have been converted from stables.

I was very impressed with the helpful and kindly hall porter and was given a very nice room overlooking the lawns. Later, he took me to meet my new boss. She was very old and wore a lot of very expensive rings. She said she liked to go to London a great deal — Harrods, Harvey Nichols, and reeled off a list. But Wednesdays we went to church at 3p.m. (Christian Scientists). The chauffeurs sat in the last row. I think I was the only one from the hotel. Their code was, only one shilling to be put in the plate — no more, no less. I was lucky I had a blue coat and skirt that had a bit of colour woven into it, of good quality, which stood up to any kind of public work. I followed the service but I was not even interested, just bored.

We returned to the hotel, which was bristling and surging with activity. For days one floor had been emptied of people being moved to other rooms. So entered the Dutch Government without their Queen, who remained with her people. Groups of them used the dining room. My employer kept strangely quiet, then suddenly she asked me to go with her to her room. I knew this was going to be an unpleasant time. She said "Daphne, I must ask you to change your mind, this war will be short and I do need you more than you think, you will be well thought of, I have no heir, no one, and you will have more than you've ever had, and you will never regret it." I said "No, I've registered as an auxiliary in the Air Force. Now the Dutch Government is here in the hotel, any moment we will be called up. We must think of our own country and defend it. The Germans are very, very well equipped. It will not be a short war. I have no inkling when we are needed or how I'll know." She looked so defeated and sad. I thought of my mother with so little, yet already belonging to this and that down in Cornwall. I had a letter from Cecil Coad (St Ives): he had volunteered for the Cornish Infantry, and Henry had joined the Navy. I then said, "Someone who has no family will be glad to drive you. She may not pass her medical." She was not listening. I left her and said goodnight. I went down to the Hall Porter and said to him, "Any news?" "Yes, would you go up to Mr. F.-S.'s room at 9 o'clock for coffee." I stared at the porter: strange, I had never spoken to Mr. F.-S. The porter said, "It is important, you must go."

I wandered around to look for Fairbanks Junior who was staying there, I always had breakfast with him. He had the next table to ours, so I always sat with him. At 9p.m. I was sitting down having coffee with Mr. F.-S.; he had a suite. He said, "Now you must be wondering why I asked you up here, but I did not want your employer to see us talking." On the radio all the forces' numbers were read out in batch numbers at certain times, which meant that we had to report to our units. The units of course were not named. The porter used to listen in over the air for the numbers given him. Mine was 880538 to unit. The porter's son was Army, and two other guests and I were to get ready to depart with Mr. F.-S. in his car when told. Two days later we were driving to London, I was dropped at Victoria Station; we had left the hotel at 4a.m. I slipped a note under the door of my employer. I thanked her for the money she gave me in advance when I turned her down, otherwise she had hardly spoken to me. She did not even go shopping.

I reported to Maidstone Barracks about 8 o'clock. About four or five of us were taken to a farmhouse and billeted in an attic. Our hosts were not very pleased. We hung around, and finally were picked up and taken to RAF Detling outside Maidstone. War had not actually been declared. We wasted four days on the farm.

PART TWO

The War Years

RAF Detling, Kent — September 1939

We presented ourselves at the Guard House, where we were signed in and taken to the WAAF quarters nearby. Originally the row of houses was married quarters. Typically one front room downstairs, then behind, the kitchen, opening on to a small garden yard with a gate on to the grass surrounding the runways and hangars — quite a way off. Up narrow stairs one front room which housed four beds, and a back-room really for one but could take two beds, and a bathroom between. The first house was empty, the upper floor was to house a cipher officer. The last house was for Miss Cope; she had served in the Army and wore a rather aged uniform and battered hat. She was fondly called Copey, always smiling and pleasant, fair and rather dumpy. She put up with a lot. Her father was a well-known watercolour artist, and I heard she was quite good. I think there was six or seven houses altogether. Our beds were three square, straw palliasses called "biscuits" put in a straight line, then two coarse cotton unbleached sheets, a pillow case and one lumpy pillow, two brown grey blankets, very prickly. Miss Cope's title was Section

Officer Cope. A Flight Officer Turner from Maidstone was over her, but lived out.

Every day, one folded up everything on to a square of three "biscuits", blankets on top. For the occasional kit inspection everything had to be laid out, but to be honest we had only a blue beret, an officer's raincoat, a red arm-band, and a black tie! The rest was to arrive eventually. I should imagine the women's part of Air Ministry had an awful time to get things going.

Our trades were a problem. Drivers were not wanted, the regular men were already full strength. However, cooking — quite determinedly — I declined; but one brave girl Joe Robbins (who was later awarded the M.M.) said yes, she would do some cooking and so was elected to do the WAAF cooking with help. I seem to remember we had a lot of scrubbing to do and window cleaning; the houses had been vacant. The next trade was Equipment: issuing of uniforms, furniture, tools, everything under the sun, in triplicate-form books. Several girls got fixed up there because men were pouring in to be equipped as well as our future 500 squadron: Avro-Ansons on recognisance from Thorney Island in the south. A few days elapsed whilst we cleaned up and other auxiliaries arrived and were shown around. First accounts office: we had to be entered for pay, forms for administration, next-of-kin; medicals at Sick Bay: a matter of formality, and some of us had had injections (tetanus) and vaccinations, with certificates. Friendships began and also were renewed and Copey allowed us to sort ourselves out. No one as yet was on any night duty; later one slept with one's shift, so as not to disturb people too much.

I do not remember the day I met Margaret Black (then Sims). I think she arrived in her Vauxhall called "Bill" with an Australian and two other New Zealanders. Margaret and I became friends until she died in 1990. She had the New Zealand flash on her shoulder. Her parents were living in Sussex at that time and were very good to me all through the war.

"Well", we said to each other, "Let's go round the camp and ask for work." Margaret went to the Accountant Officer and was employed at once. She had just finished one year at Cambridge in Science and Botany and so on. I asked to see the Medical Officer. The elderly Sergeant Thomas, old fashioned and a regular, was very dubious. The Doctor, who was Senior Medical Officer was a V.R.; he had left his general practice at Rochester, where his family lived. Dr Gross was a very good doctor and teacher. He asked me what I could do. I said I could scrub floors, make up simple medicines because I had been a photographer and had to be exact with formulas, and read ordinary Latin. I had got my St John's Certificates and I was not afraid of blood. I had inoculated some animals on the farm, but not people yet. He seemed amused at that and asked me about working with men all the time. I said, no problem at all. I would do what I was asked to do if they showed me.

When war was declared on 23 September at 11 o'clock, the sirens suddenly wailed. Being Sunday we were in the WAAF quarters and alongside was a deep trench with a ladder inside. We climbed down and I think there were ordinary school benches. Copey came down last and in the quiet chatter someone screamed and pointed. I remember saying, "It's only a spider. Don't kill him." I never realised how some people were terrified of them; in Britain we did not have any poisonous ones. The sirens then gave the all-clear. Out we came and listened to Churchill and the news on someone's radio — probably Copey's or Margaret's.

Our problem of course was clothes. We had our undies but a curious assortment of garments, thinking we would be in uniform. I had two men's white shirts, which I bought from an army surplus shop in Maidstone, and a pair of navy blue sailor's trousers. Having two white shirts I could wear my ties! I had wellingtons and heavy socks and boots from the farm days, two pullovers, and I got two white overalls from Stores. I think they were for the barber's shop, they were heavy but good for the winter. Margaret and I went off for a minor shopping spree, as Maidstone was quite near.

Soon October was over. The German aircraft used to dive in and have a nasty shoot-up along the roads. Being from a recognisance station it was important that our planes weren't shot down in action over occupied countries to examine the equipment. Our Ansons had the unenviable task of flying low and taking photographs of enemy transport movements and factions as well as airfields. About this time Assistant Section Officer Woollam arrived. She was in an immaculate Air Force uniform with a South African flash on her shoulder. She had been trained at Air Ministry as a Cipher Officer, and occupied the other end of married quarters which was nearest to the entrance to the Camp. Officer's furniture had been issued for her top floor which made a livable flat; bathroom, bedroom and living room. Downstairs the kitchen had a coal-heated stove.

Autumn was very beautiful, as the fruit orchards around were ablaze with yellow to scarlet falling leaves. The Faversham Road outlined the south-western part of the camp, renowned cherry orchards spread out.

I had settled in to a normal day, 8a.m. to 5.30p.m., walking to Sick Bay and to our quarters for meals. Some evenings when we were busy I would have a meal with the men.

Often on daylight recognisance some of the squadron were sighted and pursued; our fighters came to the rescue, resulting in casualties when the Germans shot at the aircraft. When our squadron struggled back, shrapnel and bullet wounds were attended to first before the men were taken to Chatham Hospital. The ambulance driver usually had one medical orderly with the patients. For a little while I had to be registered as a naval Sick Berth Attendant, as there were no women medical orderlies as yet. All women medical officers had the rank of Squadron Leaders. They were gradually admitted. To be a medical orderly one had to have four years training at RAF Halton, our big medical base in Bucks. When passed, you became a Leading Aircraft Man, Corporal or Sergeant. I obtained naval manuals of instruction from Chatham and studied as hard as I

107

could. I had my St John's standard book, which really only covered the basics.

Then I was given our small cupboard room for the Pharmacy, really like a large pantry. The basic medicines were limited but were made up into large Winchester bottles (one quart). The door was halved so that objects could be put on the lower half, and signatures were obtained as they were given out or taken. We had standard prescriptions for the Winchesters — most commonly used for coughs, colds, and so on. With the selections of tablets one had to be very careful in counting them out into glass tubes. Every week, I had a stock-taking for my own sake. Later on I used to be teased by officers and airmen alike with "Pearson's Pink Pills". I hasten to say we had no pink pills, it must have been something from the comics. Then we had a shocking snowy winter. Most of the airmen flaked out with a virulent flu, too sick even to report to Sick Bay. So began one of the most tiresome and exhausting times. I think there were about 40 men to each hut, a small room at the entrance for an NCO to whom I reported if we had someone on the sick list. I had every woolly on I possessed and the heavy white coat with bulging pockets, and I carried a bundle of charts under my arm. I did the simple routine of temperature, pulse, eyes, mouth, chest, and examined each bed for the right bedclothes, it was amazing how blankets were disappearing. I began at 8a.m. and barely finished when the meal trucks came. It was very rough and ready. Medicines were given out. Men had no pyjama issue, it was amazing that normally they would have them at home but they stuck to their trousers, braces slipped down. The problem was that the men slept with their arms on the braces and the arm was quite paralysed for half a day. At first it puzzled us, as all these one-armed men turned up at Sick Bay. The metal on the braces was the cause — the men sleeping on their sides, the metal pressed into an artery.

Then the M.O. sent for me and said, "I want you to study anatomy, especially all the spinal bones. The P.M.O. is coming over in about a week to give you an examination." He gave me a few other subjects to study, which I did. Then the great day came; by that time we had our ordinary uniforms, so my buttons had an extra buff up. The P.M.O. was tall and quite casual. He asked many general questions, then, out came a few bones from out of our M.O.'s drawer. He generally asked me what I did, I was careful to tell him also what I had not yet done. It was over so quickly.

About two weeks later the Commanding Officer and the Medical Officer were in the C.O.'s office and I was sent for. I nearly died when I was promoted to Corporal. Then Sergeant Thomas came in and he took me over to Sick Bay and told our mob. I felt so sorry that the men who were regulars and not corporals had not got their stripes. Then the chairman of the Corporal's Mess sent a message that I was to present myself at the Corporal's Mess to be initiated that evening. They had asked Margaret and one or two WAAF to be there. They said as I was a woman I would be initiated in a different way and gave me half a pint of beer to drink without stopping. That was easy, thus I escaped a whole pint of beer being crowned (poured over my head).

One great bonus was that Margaret's family had great friends from New Zealand, a judge and his wife, who lived in a lovely old house only one or two miles away, so we could have the luxury of hot baths. In our quarters the water never reached more than being tepid, so that was a great joy. Also, Margaret managed to get some unusual things from her parents' home to give them because we were asked at least once a week for a meal. They kept poultry. Later a law was passed that any householders within certain limits could have two pigs to breed as extra rations, but of course that meant getting enough feed for them in a healthy area. Rationing was just being introduced, with more and more limitations. In our quarters, Robbins had a dreadful time because her cooking stove for three or four could not provide for 25, so we got some bricks and cement blocks, lit a fire in the yard and had pans of baked potatoes. There were certain rations, especially for puddings, which at first was disastrous. There was the weather to cope with too. One girl called Smith helped Robbins, the carrier of the meat tins.

A recruit called Lister was initially in charge and arranged that goulash (I had never heard of it myself) was to be served, the only problem was getting enough heat out of those stoves meant to cook for four people, so the meat was only cooked partially in three different houses, it was a shambles. After several days we got some semblance of order.

Winter was passing and the spring began with the fury of the war really beginning — the Battle of Britain as it was later called. When it was sunny we could see fighter planes zig-zagging and reeling in the bright sunlight. Both our own fighters and the Germans got embroiled over us, in between our Ansons sneaked out to photograph and bomb across the channel. They carried four bombs to silence the enemy's battery attacks. There was no doubt Germany had built its forces up beyond anybody's full realisation. We were geared to think: we will defend ourselves to the end. I think that the coming of more and more Australians and New Zealanders to help was a great boost, then the Canadians and also the South Africans. In Africa and Canada there were great training camps where they taught all the new recruits to fly, whole crews. It was not for themselves: they would not be molested by Germans in those countries. The Colonials thought we were a quaint people unless they came from British parents. We were very insular; I was appalled to find we could not enroll coloured races into the Air Force, which I found out later. This had to be altered.

Then I was moved to the ground floor of the Cipher Officer's house, to enable me to be on call to get to Sick Bay. This began when I was on ward duty and personally nursed a very sick meningitis patient. The Sergeant took on the patient for part of the night, but I washed and fed him. This was for several weeks so I could not mix with people except out of doors, but not inside being in quarantine. The man mercifully died. Not long after I had another one-off patient who

111

puzzled everyone until I was sent for by the M.O. He always called me Priscilla, he said it was his favourite name. He had his microscope out, and outlined scarlet-fever skin flakes. It was the one catching "school" disease I had not had. He asked me whether I would personally look after Corporal Rosehearne, who was very ill and could not be moved, also his chest was in a bad condition. I was to be isolated from all WAAF. We went over the Corporal's body very thoroughly. The doctor took more specimens of his peeling skin and we looked at them again under the microscope. He told me I was to keep a look-out for this condition on anyone else. This very patient was an endearing man, a happily married Cornishman with three children. He died about 10 or 12 days later. I was very sad and was allowed to attend his funeral.

I managed to get a pass for Christmas and went home to Cornwall, but I do not remember very much about it. The great snow blitz ended on 14 January in Sussex next door to us, so James told me in his letter. I was writing to James, who had joined the Home Guard until he was called up. I have kept for its quaintness a typed letter and instruction for the Ansty and Cuckfield Unit. Also I note that all art galleries, their meetings, and opening days went on as usual from autumn to Christmas. James said London was desolate and dreary. My excursions since September were only with Margaret to East Hoathley on weekends off, one or two nights at the Star Hotel with Margaret's parents, and an occasional concert with the girls and airmen by lorry to another camp. I remember that our new doctor,

Dr. Norman Cust from Sydney, who seemed to have a total disregard for rank and the typical standoffishness of some of our countrymen, preferred to come with us; certainly he sang some very comic and bawdy songs and kept everyone happy. I hardly wrote to anyone but in one letter to James I said I was working very hard. I certainly had at Ditton Court Farm, so I know I did at Detling. I missed Granny Smith's meals very much. Years hence when it was all over, I kept in touch with her until she died of old age. She adored her two grandsons.

In May I was lying in bed, in fact it seemed only minutes since I fell asleep that I heard an aircraft coming in. I sat up in a second as it sounded like the engines were not right. I automatically began to pull on my jersey and navy trousers over my pyjamas. I ran out: I had on my wellingtons, socks and tin hat as I was running across the turf to the Guard Gates pushing the man on duty to the gate which he opened, he could see my red cross on my hat and heard me coming. The aircraft ploughed through the tops of the trees in the wood that lay behind the two single fields adjacent to the fenced main road. I remember landing in the nettles in the ditch, and the fearsome sight on my right of the plane on fire. I know I was battling with my boots to get there faster; it was terrifyingly hot as two crewmen coming out of the plane were dragging another man out. I turned into them and I realised that something would give. I yelled to them to run fast to the road. There was a ridge where a hedge had been routed out, I hung on to the man's harness and lay over

113

him, unfastening what I could; he was in great pain and bleeding in the face. He gasped out, "Go — full tanks and a bomb or bombs." The fierce scorching light shone on his tooth that had pushed through his cheek. All at once, the ambulance was high up on the road and men were yelling. It is strange what one does: I pulled the tooth out of the man's cheek and I knew his back or neck was severely injured and he could not be moved by me. All in seconds I put my tin hat over his face and lay over him with my elbows in the turf so as not to put any weight on him. I heard myself yelling, "Keep away, bombs and petrol aboard." There was a shocking blast, all the air in my stomach was sucked out, it seemed as if the lining had stuck together but gasping in some air finished that. I was yelling out, "Doc, over here, but keep down." I could see the flashing ambulance lights. Doc with a stretcher arrived alone at that moment. I said, "His back is injured," then another man came and his pain must have been awful as we slid him on to the stretcher. We got him over the road's barbed wire fence. The road was milling with people, they were getting the fire engines in. There was of course the ditch. I saw the C.O. helping. The first two airmen were in the ambulance for four. I crouched by my patient. I remember stripping off in sick bay and scrubbing up in the day surgery, putting on my overalls and getting into our makeshift theatre. We worked very hard getting out bits of metal from the first two men. Doc was relieving the pilot's pain and strapping him up ready to go into Chatham hospital, where they were alerted for the urgent admission. The three men were soon away.

It was 3a.m.

I felt very numb and when I got to the door the Doc. said, "I'll drive you back to your quarters." As he drove I said, "Doc., is there such a thing as night blindness? I cannot see the fire. Do I come with you to get the dead man we couldn't save? His name was Chambers." "No," Grossy said, "we'll see to that later when it's cool. I'll take you in to your room. It's quite usual after an explosion that you can't see." As he opened my front door the Cipher Officer, A.S.O.Woollam, was at the bottom of the stairs, "I've got some hot soup." I remember sitting there quietly in her sitting room. I just said thanks and went downstairs to bed. "I'll be alright for work, don't worry."

Next day I was on duty at 8a.m. in Sick Bay. I just felt tired and relieved I could see. It was only at night I could not see much. When I arrived at 8a.m. the men looked at me and said, "Don't put on your overall just yet, the M.O. wants to see you in a minute." They gave me a cup of tea. Then the M.O. came in and said, "Will you please come here a minute." To my utter surprise the C.O. of 500 Squadron and another three officers stood to attention and saluted. The C.O. stepped forward, shook my hand and made a short speech of thanks. I had to say I was very distressed that we left Chambers inside that plane and that it was all in the line of our work. I was feeling overcome. I thought I had better go to my pharmacy closet and fidget with the bottles for a while to get into stride. Strange, for three days my fear over sight continued: the M.O. said it was shock. A silly thing was, it was May and it was not dark at 5p.m. But everything settled down when the funerals were over. The pilot's aunt wrote from Surrey, such a charming letter of thanks.

As spring moved into summer the Germans were getting more aggressive, the damage in England to the main cities was appalling although people were getting used to it all.

The C.O. sent for me and said he had put me up for a commission and that soon I would be sent for by Air Ministry for training. I felt I was not being asked but told. I said, "Must I go, sir? I do not want to be an officer. I would like to be able to continue with medical work. I am studying in between." He said, "No, I am afraid not, you are to go to London for a short time. But I think they will be sending you on a course first."

As I was going out of the door I met Margaret, I could not say anything but she was to be told she had been recommended for a commission. She did not go to Air Ministry, she was to be a Cipher Officer, being good at mathematics and a partial graduate were all to the good.

Actually I was sent on a photographic interpretation course which I failed. I only did three or four days of it at Bomber Command's Headquarters. Air Chief Marshall Harris was the head, a strict but charming man. There was a serious flu epidemic. I returned to Detling, it was an event to be forgotten but endured by very sick people. To be truthful I had to attend the photographic recognition course or stay in quarters and nurse some very, very sick WAAF. Just to qualify this: these airwomen of all trades would normally be at

Headquarters as clerks, perhaps cooks, but I rang in to H.Q. reporting for duty on the phone, "I cannot leave my patients." A lorry left us food rations and I sent distress notes for medicines and medical help. I shall never, never know the procedures between Commands. We had plenty of fuel for heating. I solved my dilemma but I had missed and mucked up my course. I think that was the tightest spot, due to the fact that this event had never happened before. The lorry drivers were bemused but very kind.

Up for a Commission

I went to Air Ministry. I think I stayed at the Ex-Servicewomen's Club in Lower Sloane Street. It was cheap with good food and central for transport. I escaped going to an Officers' Training School set up later. The Air Ministry is in the same location in 1992, now the Ministry of Defence, beyond the Strand and Bush House. To me it was a marvellous area to explore, with many cheap and quick places for lunch. There were not many of us attending classes on protocol and how the RAF was run. In the past, I had always been vague about what Air Ministry meant, apart from being a controller of Air Defence. Amongst the lecturers was S/O J. Conan Doyle, a daughter of the author, a kind and highly intelligent woman with striking black hair. Our Director was Commandant Katharine Jane Trefusis-Forbes (later made a Dame), who commanded great respect from everyone and never lost her human touch. She proved to be a great liaison officer with all RAFD ruling and advisory officers. I had a great liking for her although I was not immersed in fear or awe of my senior officers as most seemed to be. I remember when her door was partly open, I peeped in, saying, "May I come in please?" I unwrapped my new shoes and said, "Don't you think they are a bargain? My uniform will be ready in only a few days. I can only afford one at first." She admired the shoes as if she always expected it. Later I was told I ought not to rush in to senior officers about my clothes — that was not on if everyone did it.

Besides, she was the highest ranking officer. I respected her but in my nature I felt she was head of a large organisation which was like a family. Much later, when I realised what diplomacy and knowledge of life she had, to face up to the government's inaction at the beginning of war must have been almost unbearable. She did have good friends amongst the RAF who knew her in the previous war.

In the early days, officers at Air Ministry must have had a very hard task to organise a great force of women in modern times in an unknown type of war, with Communists mixed up in many countries — apart from the most efficient Germany. A number of them had served in the WRAF in the last war and already had degrees, and were prominent in organisations.

For two weeks we attended talks on what Air Ministry stood for and how it worked; I was allocated to Recruitment in Victory House, next to the Air Ministry's Adastral House; there were several buildings in different branches, beginning in Kingsway.

Victory House — Recruiting in the London Blitz

Recruitment was initially formed with volunteers, but profession trades so far opened were few: drivers, clerks for equipment, stores and general work, which had been done at this time by Civil Service clerks; cooks were very much in demand. Each week there were more trades open. The problem was to fit in a mass of women eager to start training and work; some were over-trained for the menial jobs.

I interviewed, forms were filled in, then applicants were processed for medicals and finally photographed. I tried to form a pattern to fit the recruit to what she could do. So, for example, I thought a hairdresser might be good at being a dental assistant, and so on. It was a break when cooks offered to be cooks.

I was staying at the Ex-Servicewomen's Club in Sloane Street. I could walk to the No. 22 bus stop or Gloucester Street underground station, which I mostly avoided because I felt it was too closed in. I worked as late as 9p.m. All the civilian clerks left on the stroke of 5p.m. and they never worked on Saturdays.

One evening I walked out into Sloane Street and the city seemed extraordinarily quiet. Usually on a very light night with high clouds the alert would have sounded and gunfire would be shaking the houses. The only sound was the wind and a whistling whispering that turned my blood cold. It was near, yet reached far in the sky; unseen figures pressed around me. The moon burst through a gap — a balloon riding very high caught the light, a solitary wisp-like figure clung to its quilting fin, its slating cable was covered with reaching figures, arms stretched out supplicating.

Curious, I walked rapidly to an open square, the whistling filled the air until my ears were ringing with the intensity of the ghostly noise. Ant-like figures were clinging to all the cables I could see from my new vantage point. An army of ghosts. A warden passed, his war-weary face drenched with sadness.

"Warden, do you see the balloons riding high tonight?"

"Why, yes," he replied.

"Do you hear the cables in the wind?"

"Cables in the wind, no, I hear the souls of the bombed crying out for release."

"Souls of the bombed"

"Some nights they rise up and guard the city."

West Drayton — E.G.M. Award

After much bombing I was posted to West Drayton, Middlesex, half an hour from town. It was a large depot for equipping all recruits. It had been established for a long time by the men: there was even a small branch-line to the depot sheds, which housed boots and shoes, caps and badges etc. The women came in batches but we would take up to 2,000.

The RAF C.O. was Group Captain Gaskell-Blackburn, with a black beard which hid an injury; that is the only time beards were worn in the RAF. I think I came down by car; I remember the Guard-room and gates and an officer with me reported to Squadron Officer McAleary, a very pleasant middle-aged woman who received us and said, "I will send for Barnes who is the Equipment Officer, whom you'll understudy, and teach you the ropes." She rang up S/O Barnes, who came over. Thus I met Daphne Barnes, so we were Daphne B. and Daphne P. off duty; she was also Lady Barnes.

We walked through the camp, the administration area was near the main railway line; we walked down our main road towards the gates. Near on our left were our quarters, a long passage with separate rooms. My room was next to Barnes's. Batwomen were allocated to clean our rooms. Daphne B. said, "I always clean my own buttons and shoes, I advise you to do the same.". For an actress she was extraordinarily tidy and punctual and organised. I was to work in an office near the depot stores with her, and a spare table was there for an NCO when required.

As the goods came, there were masses of dockets and movement orders for goods to go to other places. You had to check signatures and go and inspect items when required or if you wanted to see for yourself.

Outside the camp there were two brick houses which housed our most senior officers, including S/O McAlery, and our mess which occupied one ground floor, a dining room (mess room), a common room, and a nice garden to relax in. We usually had dinner at 7p.m.; later the time was changed to 6.30p.m. because German bombers got wise to that and we had to give up our dinner!

As you came out of the camp, the road led down to the town's shopping area or High Street. We were only half an hour from London by road. Margaret Sims was at Heston, only five miles away so she was able to come over when she could. She was a Cipher Officer. But the intense bombing on and around London was hotting up to the point of acceptance. Beside the horror and discomfort, the actual sighting in the sky with searchlights weaving to and fro, catching a plane and keeping it in the beam so that our land-based guns could get a good aim, was spectacular. But with the everlasting noise and lack of sleep it amazes me how we dashed into London when allowed, with plenty of zest.

I wrote to my mother on 2 August 1940:

Perhaps Hitler will allow me to write, for the third time our meal was stopped again, day before yesterday and lunch, suppertime and today at 1.00p.m. D — (RAF Detling) got it pretty badly, one H — (hanger) and O — (Officers Mess) wiped out and 38 casualties, no WAAF. I got on to Colonel Sheldon last night who told me a lot . . . I may be staying there on Thursday and Friday. I am definitely having a change of air next 7 to 10 days and will send you an address when I am allowed. I shall be with Barnes and will be doing rather a concentrated job of work. At the moment we are not allowed to leave camp together, so as she has gone to see a cousin. I'm lying in the garden after our last rush to the trenches! . . . the crabs were delicious but some of it was wasted as half-way through we had a long air raid. What fun and games! I went round all the trenches and I only saw one plane. It is very hot and close after racing around, our shirts were sopping. Lunch was very cold and still there on our return . . . One girl, Grace Taylor-Wood, was at school with me and at St Lukes (Hospital) when I had my tonsils out, she came through as a recruit this week. Had tea in peace — must go up to camp now. Let me know how much the crabs were, they were very fresh.

I must explain without drawing a map how the trenches were placed. All the sleeping huts for airwomen were grouped to the right of the centre of the camp, mostly spaced about 40 feet apart. Coming in from West Drayton itself were two guard gates and a house on the right. On the left of the public road was the requisitioned WAAF Officers' Mess. When you entered the RAF station gates, a decent space down, were our sleeping quarters. We got around on bicycles but some officers like Barnes, Derrick and so on, had their cars. Barnes had a Bentley and to my great joy I was allowed to drive it when we went to London later on. Margaret still had her Vauxhall "Bill".

On the left of the centre of the camp were all the administrative offices, a world of paperwork and accounts; at the farthest end were the kitchens, sergeants' and airwomen's messes and in the furthest western corner the RAF Officers' Messes. To be honest I hardly saw any RAF Officers except the Commanding Officer because women had replaced the men, or were 30 to one.

Now comes the event which changed the whole of my life. I typed a letter in an official envelope but stamped and posted it in Uxbridge — someone must have posted it for me to my mother.

Air Ministry have just rang up to say that I have got the King's Medal in the Military Division but

125

it will not be published for a day or two, but I am allowed to tell you. Apparently it will be in the papers in 48 hours. This is very disturbing for my evening work. Margaret will be here for dinner tonight so I shall have to hurry . . . D — (Detling) has been bombed but not badly I think. I had a most enjoyable time in town with Margaret Chamberlain, although it was only for 24 hours. (*Margaret's brother was the actor Richard Chamberlain.*)

We went to town and saw the Leyfeldts at Richmond. They were awfully pleased to see us. (*Originally they were friends of Audrey Pearson in Clifton and became lifetime friends of mine, the Vitry family were the ones we visited in Paris.*) You remember Mrs. Vitry in Paris? Apparently they all left for their house in Tours and have not been seen since. London may well be Paris, the streets are simply crowded with French people. We had a cocktail party in the RAF Officers' Mess last night, what a time we had. It was to celebrate the C.O.'s fifth year in W.D. (West Drayton).

I was very pleased to get the papers. I have £14 in hand up to June and another £11 coming in on the 30th and I do not actually spend much here. The C.S.A. is hefty (Civil Service Stores) but considering I had to get a full set of underclothes, stockings and shirts as I had to give everything in before I left D — . . . also the sports outfit was costly . . . the daisies were quite fresh and they look so nice in my room. Margaret S — (Sims) has just rung up to ask me to the theatre. It's only 25-30 minutes run from town.

The Air Ministry announcement was made and confirmed. The Press release was on 18 August. I sent a telegram to my mother to say that I was being interviewed and it would be broadcast on that day.

It would be a day or barely two days later. I had a pile of invoices to countersign; there had been both incoming and outgoing goods which I had promised to do for the N.C.O., who had the biggest burden of dispatching; if officers did not keep up they were blamed. So I asked my WAAF C.O. to excuse me from dinner early to speed down into camp to the office. I had barely sat down when the phone rang and Air Ministry was on the line. I think it was Commandant (now Air Commodore) Trefusis-Forbes herself, who had been put through from the Mess to say at this moment on the radio, Winston Churchill was announcing in Parliament the award of the Empire Gallantry Medal, Military Division, to me. I felt very dazed, but not for long. I had no time to sign more papers when airwomen and some officers burst in and I was hauled back to the mess.

I do not remember if there was an air raid or not. Early in the morning Air Ministry Public Relations Officers, both WAAF and RAF, were down before breakfast and I was driven into the camp. The Press were later scrutinised and escorted to a small tent with a table and a few chairs. I was briefed carefully and was to rest in the tent after each session. I remember reading a lot of material about recruiting. I began to get into a really petrified mess. Barnes was not there. I suppose she was signing forms, but she could be formidable if she thought I was being over-used.

Anyway, I thought the Germans would soon be there and they were worse. One climbed down into so many trenches and quietly looked down the lines to see if someone was ill or temperamental; our job with our N.C.O.s was to deal with things the best we could. People had lost their homes, parents and children were evacuated into the country.

There were several climaxes within the women's sector, because the WAAF were not integrated into the Air Force Act. So much had to be done as numbers of women were leaving. To use Squadron Leader Beryl Escott's words in her admirable book, *Women in Air Force Blue*, the wastage was 27 per cent overall. So an airwoman could just leave and no legal action could be taken. By April things began to improve. We were given the same badges of rank, re-mustered and classified the same as the RAF under equal orders. This rebounded on me by the decoration E.G.M. conferred on me, because it was a useful tool in a way for the Air Ministry to encourage WAAF to join up in "War Weapons Work."

My mother came up for my investiture and stayed in the Mess for the occasion. Barnes drove us to Buckingham Palace. She was my other guest. I remember it was a scorching hot day. Daphne B. and mother sat in the centre party facing the dais. Myself, and some others were being instructed by marching in

128

from the left to a certain spot, which was easy, the carpet was red but deeply patterned. Then, opposite the King, one smartly turned left to face him, and took so many paces forward so that he did not have to move to pin the decoration on. To my distress I had to curtsey in uniform and not salute like the men. It is still the custom. There were quite a lot of decorations being awarded. At the end we, with our relatives and friends, went out, and in the quadrangle others joined us. Daphne B.'s husband, Sir Kenneth Barnes, took us to the Ivy Restaurant, of renown to actors. We met some very interesting people. Kenneth was the Director of ENSA (Entertainments National Service Association).

Mother returned to Cornwall the next day, I only remember the heat. Then the next month a Liaison Officer from the Air Ministry took me to Malvern, where I was to have my portrait painted by Dame Laura Knight. She was on the Official Artists list.

Dame
Laura Knight, RA,
War Artist

I quote from a letter written on 31 August 1940 to my
mother. The address I wrote from was the British Camp
Hotel, Wynds Point, Malvern, in a lovely place next to
J.M. Barrie's home. Dame Laura used his garden for a
studio, with a lovely backdrop of the Malvern hills. I
was concerned when we heard on the news that:

18 London districts had been bombed, still we
have them here (German planes) over all night and
I was startled with the house shaking and vibrating.
Floyd is up here with me which makes life more
amusing. I am being painted in a tin helmet holding
a rifle. Air Min. will be furious but Dame Laura
says my helmet looks like a bonnet effect on the
back of my head and the rifle makes a good line.
WAAFs are not to carry arms. Controversy is still
raging and this will upset the apple cart. Dame
Laura is still adamant and firm. I say if Germans
kill women and children deliberately in their

homes and in the streets, machine gunning, then the women must be prepared to kill to protect their children. Machines are coming down in remote places and streets . . . Floyd is ringing up Uncle George (he lived in Cheltenham) to come to dinner. Last night we went past Muriel Bell's puppets and saw her husband Waldo, he looks like a puppet himself, a most curious fellow. We are seeing his show tonight. I sit (for Dame Laura) from quarter to eleven until 5.30 and I'm getting quite sun burnt. Scott Sunderland, the actor, is with Sir Barrie; he was in the Pygmalion film and in Barretts of Wimpole Street play. I must go, Dame Laura is coming out of her studio.

We were there about six to seven days. I liked Dame Laura very much and later she used to write to me. Her husband Charles Knight was a quite different personality. He was very formal in dress. He was a portrait painter and got a very enameled finish with his paint.

I don't remember returning, only that it had been wonderful in the sun, with pre-war meals and civilised and charming people, including the owners and staff at the hotel.

The irony of the gun was over-ruled by using a gas mask, in truth no way would one open up a gas mask in such an artistic manner. Most of us voluntarily attended gun practice with Enfield 103s. Later, not long after, we were allowed to carry revolvers. James later gave me one and taught me to use a Smith-Wesson which was very heavy.

131

Harrogate

The Germans knew we were moving the camp of recruits and to avoid a slaughter, suddenly with great speed everyone was numbered into train batches, West Drayton to London, to Harrogate. At that time I began to have shocking stomach pains and headaches. I thought, I must not say anything until we get to Harrogate. I was in the last batch but one and was in charge of one train load, with an RAF Sergeant, WAAF Sergeant and Corporals. The last kitchens had packed our rations for the journey. When we got to Harrogate Station it was pouring with rain. The trucks were only for our kitbags and cases, and we had to march from the station to a large hotel up an awful hill. I tried not to be ill, so I said to the Sergeant, "Shall we sing our way up?" I felt we were not doing so badly until an RAF car glided up and an angry RAF officer said, "We've not won the war yet, stop that singing." We were marching in time. I told the N.C.O.s I was halting the march and I did, then said, "Five minutes rest and we are ordered not to sing." We dripped, batch by batch, into the Grand Hotel, Harrogate, and reported. I reported to a Squadron Officer Swaffley, she was grim and tired. She said the usual things in greetings, we

were occupying three of the largest hotels and classes
had been arranged for the recruits. She reminded me
that women never sang during marching. I muttered, "I
am sorry, ma'am, we were all a bit miserable." I am
sure that rule is not down in A.M.O.s (Air Ministry
Orders). I was given a nice room with a telephone. I
signed myself out for dinner in the Mess and went to
bed. I struggled for two days, then at 1a.m. in the third
night I was in desperate pain, I rang the Medical
Officer S/Leader Butler-Jones, a very good M.O.

She was round in minutes, she rang for an
ambulance, collected my toiletries and said, "A ripe
appendicectomy." I was operated on apparently almost
immediately, but there was more to come. I was
unconscious for four days. The Germans were being a
nuisance. When I opened my eyes everything was
blurred, then I had a visit from Air Commandant
Trefusis-Forbes. Her braid of gold laurel leaves on her
cap was all blurred. I said, "Ma'am, it's you, I'm better.
Thank you", and she sat for a while, with sister fussing.
Then S/Leader Swaffley sent me a case of quarter-
bottles of champagne. I was very weak and they asked
about my mother. I remember saying, "I'll write when I
can; say I'm sick but all right. Don't let her come, it's
too dangerous." I think I felt helpless. Then a sister
came and put a large red card on the back of my
bedhead. I said, "The raid is taking a long time?" and
she replied, "You are to remain still. The hospital is
being evacuated except for you and three other male
patients. You will be looked after." Four to six sisters
stayed with us; the men's ward was on the same floor,

so we were together. Bombs were dropping very close. I think I am correct that part of the kitchen quarters was damaged. All the patients were eventually returned, no-one was hurt or killed, but there was a good bit of clearing up to do. I cannot thank those sisters enough for quietly looking after us, though we begged them to go.

Later I had quite a bit of sick leave. Margaret wrote to the depot and said her father's partners at Bradford would be delighted to have me. I stayed with them for a week. They owned half of a Bradford Mill, called "Triffits", where they spun the New Zealand and Australian wools for uniforms. They were real Yorkshire people, hospitable. regarding food, the custom was to have supper at 10p.m., apple pie and cream!

When I was well enough I returned to the depot. I wrote to my mother:

I was given a very nice room in which were lovely roses, carnations and cyclamen. A nice fire! The view overlooked the foggy town of Harrogate . . . To my joy Marjorie Turner arrived in the afternoon for the night (F/Officer Turner now Squadron Officer) she was the area WAAF Officer over S.O. Cope at Detling. Dame Laura Knight has written. Clare of course and her mother (the Dores at Liss)). I miss my nurses very much. One, Honor Capill, is coming to tea today. She was at school with the Ticehursts (my cousins). Foster, another nurse, her mother has invited me out to her home 6 miles from here. I still miss Barnes dreadfully, she has wired and written a lot. She is attached to an Air Ministry unit and billets herself at Esher . . . Floyd has written every day and sent me a book called "The Spotten Lion", by Gander Dower, it promises to be good. Margaret Sims of course writes often. Had letters from Detling, not a building standing whole now and everyone is billeted out. Not a WAAF killed though several hurt . . .

War Weapons Week and Recruiting

The London officials were quick off the mark to embroil me in War Weapons Week. I asked to go to London, and then on to Cuckfield.

Another letter to my mother:

My Dear M. This won't be a very long letter, there is not much news. I went down to Cuckfield to have a breath of air, I did not do very much as I went Saturday evening and returned Sunday evening. Mrs. Williams was there with John (wife and son of Floyd's ex-batman) and the dogs were very pleased. By now you will have received my wire — up to the present I'm to do Cornish recruiting for eight or nine days as it is St Ives and Penzance War Weapons Week. If it is not cancelled I will come down by train on Thursday, the 24th and look around and confirm arrangements on Friday. On Saturday I'll be present at the opening of the War Weapons (week), St Ives. In the evening I'll attend a dinner and meeting and Boxing Match at St. Ives.

Monday, Tuesday, Wednesday and Thursday I'll do Penzance and St Ives alternately, noting their half days. Friday, St Just and district. Helston begin their Weapons Week on Saturday and I'll do (the) district there. Now this is the strange part, my driver is David Lindner (Uncle Moffat's great nephew) and he could stay with the Lindners! and I have a Corporal and possibly another officer as I may have to rest a bit. Of course knowing Air Ministry all this is likely to be cancelled at any time. Another thing has happened, I'm now in the Security and help with the RAF CID people with odd things. I'm being sworn in on something on Monday and given my first job which is not too easy. I have to know all the plain clothes women and work mainly with them connected with Fifth Columnists and people in uniform.

Our recruiting business is huge, and taking all aliens in, causes the detective business to leap up. If I get dug in there it may mean help for a regular job after the war.

What do you think of us all receiving the King's Commission; it's too amazing and sudden. It means no one in the Service can get out and that men take orders from us, if airmen, and have to salute. So far I don't see any difference!

I returned to town but did not finish the letter. I added:

Floyd has written from his battery saying he had a very hot time. The medical officer is pleased with me and I can continue. Can you test Mrs. Berryman (the farmers wife next door to my mother) whether she can put Corporal Chapman and me up at the farm, giving us breakfast and perhaps supper most evenings. Lunch and tea we'll have at work. Ousley the other officer will have to billet in the town. I do not know her very well, she is elderly with white hair. Chapman is charming and we get on with work smoothly. David fetches us in the mornings, so if you want your shopping or anything else fetched, we can fit it in. Did you get the cheese? I got it at Cuckfield, he (the shopkeeper) was so aghast at the thought of "only" a pound. He gave it me as if I asked for a world tour. I find even in London food is tiresome — the lack of fruit and the same old dishes is to be expected. In the restaurants they are extraordinarily resourceful but everywhere is very dear. It's rare to get an ordinary lunch under 2/6 without a tip. I sent (you) some sugar, two apples, and *Battle of Britain*. Hope they will be intact. I can never get hold of string, paper and boxes at the same time. We had a very rowdy night, only guns but no sleep until 5a.m., the guns are louder than bombs. Of course, what I've mentioned about security business is between us. I hope to be down on the 24th, with love to you and don't get too tired with Aunt G.! (*Aunt Grace was staying with my mother.*)

I should mention mother had no telephone and the Berryman's phone was our lifeline, offered freely. Of course we paid for our calls. Also the people I sent down to stay for a week or two was extra revenue for them, and an interest for my mother. There were a number of WAAF whose losses were pretty shattering and Cornwall was an ideal place to walk, think and be given time to mend their lives. My various cousins used to stay, but the biggest problem for them was the food rationing. Certainly there was plenty of milk, and eggs to a point. Mother joined in with the church, Red Cross and local enterprises, there was plenty to do. Also visiting out-of-the-way cottages where some of the old were. Hence the mention of many people going to Cornwall for recuperation.

After returning to Air Ministry's Victory House I had to go up to Harrogate to have a medical after the operation; it is a surgical routine. That over, I was met by Daphne Barnes at the Station. She was very pleased to see me, I think she felt that she had thankfully missed out on that horrible trek to the north and never knew I was feeling pretty awful at the time. We were to meet Margaret Sims at the Grosvenor House Hotel in Park Lane for tea. Margaret was a bit late, but we all talked our heads off. Daphne B. was asked to stay for dinner but she had to have dinner with Kenneth. I remarked in a letter to my mother that London is packed and the Grosvenor was full of foreigners and especially Jews. Margaret said it was like Amsterdam where she had been when just before she joined us at Detling. Margaret made me stay in bed late, her

139

parents and Margaret were asked to an Empire luncheon. I was to appear to be a New Zealander or South African, as the chief guest was Sir Cyril Newall. All I remember about it was that Margaret's father kept introducing me to people. He was so proud of me that I told Margaret she must quieten him down. She just smiled, "You can't tell Pa anything." We returned to the hotel; we only had two warnings, traffic noise was the only sound. Margaret driving, we all left for East Hoathley. The Sims had invited me for four to six weeks but I accepted for two weeks and got really fit, then went down to my mother. In Sussex, before going home, it was bitterly cold and frosty, and very high up we saw terrific dog fights but never knew which was what, one saw great trails of white condensation. At 10.30a.m. there were two bangs and an airman flopped out three fields away, his Spitfire in the wood nearby. Margaret returned to RAF Heston, but being near came home often. There were quite a few New Zealanders staying here on leave, amongst them, the Horsleys, he was a surgeon, and his wife, Irene, I had met before. I had breakfast in bed and after lunch I had to rest, but I was getting stronger. I was to be with my mother within two weeks for Christmas in Cornwall. It was great to be home. Mother was still at Trewan, St Ives.

I do not remember that Christmas but we would have caught the bus outside the farmhouse and visited St Ives and Penzance. I was still not 100 per cent fit.

I returned to London and wrote:

When I saw London I was amazed at the damage caused by the night before.

Back to London — New Home Billet, the Blitz

On 26 January 1941 I arrived in London some days before writing to Cornwall where I had Christmas and leave:

I have been in a whirl; I stayed with Margaret at Claridges and the following morning went to the National Gallery and saw the picture (Laura Knight's portrait of me) which was labelled wrongly. I called in at Air Ministry on the way to the station where I met the Director (Commandant Trefusis-Forbes), who told me I was posted to Victory House, so I reported and had to stay the night. Then on Saturday morning I was told to report to Harrogate, so I dashed up by the midday train. On the Sunday I was passed medically fit subject to the hospital surgeon examining me, so I had to wait until Tuesday for that. I'm not allowed to stay very long but they were letting me stay here until I settle finally. The next thing is to return to Victory House (it is attached to the large building of Air Ministry called Adastral House). A Countess Ougier d'Ivry has called, introduced to me by Baroness Bauche who takes in paying guests, she would take me for £2.2.0 a week but frankly that is too much, I know that would mean £2.10.0 in the end.

Here I would add I would always be out for lunch and evening meal times. I was back for the moment at the Ex-Servicewomen's Club. I remember going with the Countess to her flat one evening, having coffee, a beautifully furnished place with lovely pictures and exquisite pieces. She told me quite frankly she was away a lot on government work, she was very direct but discreet. I did not ask any questions. I casually mentioned the Vitrys vanishing from Paris and their home in Tours. Our eyes met several times and I was convinced she was in SOE, so I wondered about Baroness Bouche too. I write this in passing.

When I left early from Victory House, 4.30p.m., I had a lot to think about. I was going to meet Irene Vanbrugh, the actress, sister of Kenneth Barnes. She misses her sister Violet very much. The Vanbrugh sisters were very much loved and always played to full houses. Irene had a charming flat not far from Marble Arch, and sometimes when in town I had afternoon tea with her at 4p.m. I remember her beautiful china, hoping it would never get smashed up.

I had better at this stage mention I was living at St John's Wood. Some while ago Daphne B. mentioned that if I could think it over, she and Kenneth are amicably separated but in fact tied by their son, Michael, who was continuing his schooling in Canada. The law did not allow people who were not disabled to have two servants for one person in one house, but if I were living there, the housemaid would be willing to work in the postal sorting office during the day and the cook, Lily, who was much older, could go on as usual, and both the women would have their wages and a home. Underneath the house there was a reinforced air-raid shelter and all mod-cons.

I wrote to my mother from Acacia Road, St Johns Wood, NW:

I have just moved in to my new quarters after tea today. Nellie welcomed me and had a really nice dinner ready. I have two rooms, one in the basement and the other on the second floor. Kenneth returns tomorrow. Barnes will be up at the end of the week. I shall have my evening meal well cooked and regularly at 7p.m., then milk at 9.30. Breakfast at 8a.m., a car from ENSA to drive me to Victory House and if I am ready to leave work at 5.30p.m., be able to get a lift back or at 6p.m. (ENSA is in Drury Lane, and easy to walk through into Kingsway), including weekends, 30/- a week. My French Countess wanted £2.2.0. We are allowed 35/- per week for billeting, though of course, no messing bills, which average £5/-/- per month, although we may receive £2/-/- in the future. I'm getting several invitations but cannot always accept them. Yesterday Alec was making a speech at the Overseas HQ, and a reception was being made for Dominions Officers. As I was supposed to be off duty at 1p.m. I had arranged to meet them at the Cumberland. Well things went wrong, and we all had a hilarious lunch at 3p.m. Going without food gave me such a pain and I was so tired I had to ring Alec up and say I could not go. Anyway I had dinner with him at the Berkeley, he rang up here before I moved in, asking me.

So I left the Ex-Servicewomen's Club. I missed seeing the odd friend or cousin coming through. The beds were comfortable, it was for all ranks, and licensed. So I returned this time to No. 35 Acacia Road, St John's Wood. I stayed with Daphne B. (referred to as Barnes outside the house) on many occasions. Also, Kenneth said he would be grateful if I took on the job of hostess when I was free and he would give me warnings of his small dinner parties. Cook was delighted because she missed Daphne B's social guidance over food. No more ringing up Harrods, or any provision shop; being in the Strand, I might easily find the odd delight near Covent Garden.

When I returned from Cornwall, the first morning's work saw me at the office in charge. Deferred service started on Wednesday and I had not studied Air Ministry Orders or the newspapers very much. I felt that orders, and more orders, were never going to end. I wondered if I would ever get strong again. I knew there would be a great deal of walking to do if the

Germans could not be stopped strafing the roads and toppling buildings over into the main streets. This was the time families gathered up their rugs and night belongings to take up their positions on the back of the underground platforms.

I could not have entered into the work force at a busier time: Dunkirk had happened; women were being enrolled into more trades and sent home for call-up. Combined recruiting centres were being organised throughout Britain, and Victory House remained the London recruiting centre. So first off I found myself attached to Harrogate for three days. I left on Sunday at 11.10a.m., so I missed the Czech Club reception for the services. I was invited to be the Czech Liaison Officer; I suppose it was remembered I stuck up for them when they were invaded.

Anyway I rang Cornwall to see if my mother was all right. I had to partake in a terrific march past in aid of War Weapons Week.

I wrote:

London is in a frightful mess. Today I will go to Ardwicke with Heywood on a duty run with the CEO. We start at 08.25a.m. and return after tea. One (place) is on the East coast and the other in part of Manchester. Apparently we are in the centre of England . . . I had a very tiring run to Leeds, Huddersfield, Oldham and Rochdale and finally Manchester, returned at 10p.m. Very fruitful journey though the country is very foggy, mountainous hills, covered with emerald green turf, all black and sooty soil peeping out and black walls. Houses are all black and sooty, even in the country. Miles and miles of chimneys and factories and sordid streets packed with people. One never saw the sky even in the dales. Will post this and hope for the best.

Returning to London I wrote:

Looking at the evening papers I see LONDON BOMBED in large headlines. In spite of the fact of working in the City, I'm not conscious of it; alerts and all clears go off amid the traffic roar. At nights guns bumble away and planes drone in the distance, but so far nothing to bother about. Have had a fiendish cold all week and now seeing daylight. Saturday, after lunch, I am going over to a balloon centre to see how they are made and repaired. It is a very tricky job and recruits have to be very tough. Unless one has seen it done, it is very difficult to describe. On Sunday F/O Rimington has offered to take me out to the country to some stables in Harpenden (Herts) to see friends.

Apparently everyone hates recruiting and very few officers remain . . . the department certainly gets more curses than thanks.

Found you some dried bananas today.

I mentioned in the same letter that two of my cousins were joining up in Liverpool. Both had their home in

147

Cheltenham so I can only surmise that they were visiting our Uncle Charlie's wife, Aunt Lotty. Their two sons Brian and Charles were younger than us, and Grace was the only daughter.

Work is pretty hectic at the moment; recruits are pouring in from all directions. The doctor at Victory House is very nice and is keeping an eye on me; we all get very weary. When I left Harrogate, it was completely snowed up with drifts up to 10 feet lying across the roads.

Barnes is still at Kenley. My officers are nice to work with, Flight Officer Rimington and Squadron Officer Hackforth-Jones (the author of adventure stories).

My mother received a long letter from Mrs. Bywater-Ward, the mother of Angela who stayed with us in the Isle of Wight whilst her parents were in Malta and Gibraltar. Mrs. B.-W. was very generous in her praise of my incident and delighted over the portrait, especially as I was in uniform. She lived in Exeter and described all the evacuees and the saving up of rations for cakes and whatever for Christmas.

BBC —
"In Town Tonight"

I wrote to my mother from St Johns Wood, postmarked 11 February 1941:

My Dear M. Do you remember saying "I wonder whether you'll ever do 'In Town Tonight?' " Well I was on the air last night and this morning. Only one had to say exactly what was written and not much choice; odd words I was allowed to correct. So we had five rehearsals and I got colder and colder and at 6.15p.m. I could not stand it any more and said I must have a drink — this was hailed with great cheer — so Hanbury (the S.O.) and the Sergeant with Elizabeth Cowell, Bruce Belfridge, Roy Rich and Keith (BBC reporters) rolled into the nearest pub and I drank three brandies and ginger ale before I could warm up. Elizabeth (Cowell) was at another table, I think you are right you may not like her, she is very sophisticated and I should imagine a little spoilt. However, she was very decent to me and we are going out next week to a show. Bruce Belfridge is very pale and round faced, young and flat-expressioned, not very tall. Roy Rich is very plain with glasses and fools around all the time. After the show I met Margaret (Sims) Betty Mackay and Josephine Cardew at the Sloane St Club where we had supper.

Next day I went down to Kenley to see Barnes. Had lunch in the RAF Mess then she drove me down to Wasp Green Farm, south of Redhill, where some old friends of hers were. Sybil Crossley is a singer and broadcaster — her usual occupation is to run a very difficult milk round and milk the cows. The others, Mrs. Fagen with two landgirls and one gardener, do it all themselves. 80 High E. bombs have fallen on this small country village, killing some of their cows and a horse.

Have just listened to Winston Churchill and his speech — he seemed rather tired and not so snappy.

Recruiting is getting very hectic. Yesterday I felt pretty rotten and everyone was very decent (to me) and now I don't begin work until 10a.m., which makes a world of difference — I don't feel so tired now Kenneth has returned today. I go with him all the way by car. Saves energy and fares, which are simply awful. Buses are rather bad in this direction and to save being late when the eighth or ninth bus has passed full up, one gets a taxi; I'm trying to get you some oranges . . . I wonder whether you got the tin of mixed sweets and later the slabs of chocolate, I was amazed when I came across the latter only 2/8 per lb.

I then go on telling my mother about Alec Beecham, M.P. for West Penrith, Cornwall; I remember how I met him on the Penzance train to London at lunch; it was arranged that in the future I could take a bus ride to the House of Commons, where I could have a quick lunch with him. I did not realise how fond he was going to become of me. Also, I rather felt he was just a civil servant once elected by the people. He stood for the National Liberals, which were in country or remote seats; for wartime they were aligned with the Conservatives.

I did tell him I was very alarmed at the wrangling and corruption in the civil service. It was very difficult to be in conflict with a civil service which would not hasten the process in a crisis. The Germans were not going to hover over us whilst the civil servant of the time went through a rigmarole to get an order or letter done, so whilst queues of volunteers/conscripts waited and waited, and we processed on, the clerks up and went home on the dot. Whilst I interviewed people coming in from the street, the evening papers would announce a trade which was not open yet, or make ludicrous statements of which we could not trace the origin. No one seemed to know what the other was doing; the press relations department was in another building and probably had never seen a recruiting officer but kept putting out amazing statements which we could not support.

WAAF May Carry Arms

Squadron Officer Hackforth-Jones was the C.O. of all recruiting areas and worked on one floor. Flight Officer Rimington was C.O. of London Recruiting and was next to my room with S.O. Holmes. I interviewed people and answered queries, whilst A.S.O. Tebbs, Coles and King came and relieved me at meal times and rush hours. I was also supposed to be understudying Holmes.

I wrote to my mother:

As I was free after work Rimington suggested taking her car out. We met Margaret Sims and Betty Mackay, had supper in Leicester Square, and arranged to go down to Sussex on Saturday. Saturday morning was lovely; we had to motor through Henley where Barnes is stationed, so we had lunch in the mess there. Then sailed on to East Hoathley (Margaret's home), where we stalked rabbits with guns until dark. Sunday proved wet, but the Reeds, Dr. Maclean and Irene, and John Hemsley came over — it was nice seeing them all again. We drove back and Rimington insisted on my staying the night at Streatham where she lived, so I could drive to work in the early morning. On Wednesday we are going to the N.Z. Club to a *Thé Dansant* until 7p.m. Alec is coming here (St Johns Wood) to dinner (he gets on well with Kenneth who likes to be up to date with politics). It has come out in orders that the WAAF may carry arms. (I think that urged us on to practice on rabbits, being useful too for the Sims larder, which gets stretched with all the New Zealanders and us).

Margaret Sims was actually born in Surrey and eventually went to school in England. Her parents lived in Christchurch, New Zealand; her father was a pastoralist, owned meat factories and ice works. He had studied very hard from his boyhood. When I knew them they had sailed to and fro between Australasia and England. Mrs. Sims was born in Scotland; she was a very quiet and gentle woman, a very talented pianist and a good hostess. All through the war they took in many New Zealand airmen who were on sick leave, their house was always open to their friends who stayed on in England when war broke out. East Hoathley was a delightful Sussex village; their home was much bigger than it looked — an extensive garden and lovely young wood plantation on one side, and several fields.

They all went to church at 11.00a.m. on Sunday when home. By road there was quick access to London, especially the West, convenient for Margaret at Heston.

153

I wrote to my mother on 24 February 1941:

I'm glad you received the chocolate etc. all right. I am trying to secure some canned marmalade from the milkman; Seville Oranges are hopeless at present. Mr. Sims is interested himself in your carrot marmalade from a commercial point of view, so could you send him a pot as he wants to experiment with it. I met Hugh Smith (Ditton) who was passing through London; he is working on carrots at the lab. (West Malling Research Station), trying to put them into cold storage after the apples come out. At the moment there is a glut of carrots, so perhaps Mr. Sims' money, interest and glut might hit off a good thing.

Flood of Enrolments, Incendiary Bombs

Recruiting is fast and furious and I'm anxious for the WAAF who are already in, as the expansion is too rapid in my opinion to cope with the complications that arise, from unexpected conditions for new troops, undisciplined; also, junior officers who are not always capable enough to handle older women. As this war is going to be long, and no serious cases have come up already, we must be prepared to cope. The ATS have crumbled altogether and have come pouring into us for enrolments. We cannot take them. It's all too sad. The RAF itself is a grand Service but its administrative side leaves a lot to be desired. All orders are issued from Air Ministry civilians. A civil servant cannot be dismissed if he or she has served one year unless she has done a crime worthy of court proceedings. So the indifference and wastage are truly awful. I'm coming off actual interviewing tomorrow and will be learning S/O Holmes' job which is all clerical work, calling people up and assessing trades. Kenneth is away until Monday. He is very nervous of raids and fusses a bit when the guns go off (we are very near Primrose Hill battery).

The day before yesterday a German plane skimmed over the balloons, the marks clearly visible. The raids are very short and the defences very good and soon scatter the enemy.

The Balkan situation is damnably serious. I wish the Grecian women and children could be evacuated to Africa. Our own English people should have gone to Canada much more.

Aunt Gussie wrote and told me about poor Henry (he was our St Ives studio boy) I was very upset. (I did not know at this time he was on the HMS *Hunter*, it sank so quickly). So many have gone now. I heard a South West town had some bombs dropped this morning.

On Tuesday, Rimington took me at lunchtime to the Bank of England where I saw over several departments, and they opened up one of the vaults, where we were shown crowns and silver sets and coins of the year of my birth. I was asked to come again and would be shown Treasury notes and forgeries I also saw the vast crater where the underground station was wiped out of existence and debris was still being craned up, where 300 bodies had been removed. These underground shelters are pure death traps. Similar things happened near Streatham, where the mains burst. I have now learnt that the bombing of Aylesford

Paper Mills caused one and a quarter million pounds of damage, but only two men were killed.

The new incendiary bomb now dropping explodes with some force after two and a half minutes. They drop in hundreds and these London kids of 10 to 14 put them out with great pluck, putting them in buckets of water. Also the women here stand up to the raids much more than the men, who seemed to be stunned and dither. The United Dairies at the top of the road (St Johns Wood) have huge stables and the other week an H.E. dropped with masses of incendiaries and left the stables burning. A shorthand-typist chopped the halters and freed them, other female staff got every horse out unscathed. Except for the police, there were no men about.

The uneducated man seems to have no guts at all in a crisis; these charwomen and working-class women who always had to fight seem to be magnificent in a raid.

I hope you are getting enough to eat. I'm saving my sugar in the office, we are allowed four lumps a day.

Bombing of Buckingham Palace and Café de Paris (Café Royal)

I wrote to my mother in March 1941:

> I went down to Cookham by train on Saturday, I was all the morning getting there; Joy, wife of Hugh Smith, and Sonia their daughter met me. Hugh joined us later at a small hotel in the village. I returned by bus to Maidenhead and fast train to London. I don't know why but I was very tired and in spite of every gun in London going off and the house shaking, I got into bed and fell sound asleep amidst the unholy row and apparently slept through the All Clear, two more raids, the alerts and All Clears. On the way to work I went past Buckingham Palace, the colonnade front with a lodge-like place across the road has been bombed to pieces, railings torn down and a huge crater.

The first Palace bombing began in September. The Café de Paris was the restaurant described in the paper in Regent Street, a very nice place (later called the Café Royale), about 40 service people were killed, high rankers being rather an expensive place. It had a lovely floor and a good cabaret.

I'm dining with Margaret on Thursday, and Alec on Wednesday. He has been given a marvellous job, I can't think what it is. Must go to sleep as I have to go early to the office. You must take care with your fainting attacks, I'm sure you walk and garden too much and dash at things. Probably lifting buckets of water too. Wish you could get somewhere else.

I received a letter that my mother had a bad chill, and on 15 March I advised her to cancel all her arrangements. She must have asked me about the weather in London and I replied:

Of course it's cold walking to and fro to lunch and walking to the garage (where Kenneth's car is kept), and walking for a bus in the evening, otherwise I hardly know it's winter. Hot air and electric light are on all day. At night I sleep with my window wide open and it saves me.

By now you will have received my letter about last weekend. Actually now planes are overhead but there is a thick fog so soupy I have a shrewd suspicion it's a smoke screen, as it is a full moon.

It's like the near guns of France in the last war we used to hear in the Isle of Wight only much accentuated.

No National bread in London on sale yet. There's a scarcity of jam though. The restaurant which was hit was the Café de Paris near Piccadilly and the Palace, you would have seen it in the Telegraph. I saw it on Monday, a stick of bombs fell. A miracle they missed the centre of the building, several fell in the courtyard where we put the car another two on the other side by the Lodge. The London Shoe Shop, a branch of the one we saw in Paris, near Sloane Street Club, was quite blown out and I'd just sent Hugh Smith there to get some shoes the morning after. The crocuses in Regents Park are a blaze of yellow and in Hyde Park a stream of purple.

I don't think I'm anywhere thrilling, in fact it's an ordinary city clerk's life and dreadful after a station (RAF). I was posted to Newcastle for three weeks on Monday, and owing to my leave, they cancelled it, they said as I had been working hard, I must take all the leave owing. I am very well really, have shaken off the cold, not missed work one single day.

Dinner with Alec Wednesday, Kenneth was asked, Ray Squires (Home Office) was there, and Geoffrey Shakespeare, M.P., descendent of Will Shakespeare's brother, and his wife. Thursday I had Margaret to lunch and she asked me to dine, where I met Elizabeth Hockey, a WAAF Officer and three other Australians.

Friday was a day of surprises: F.O. Rimington turned up with a boyfriend, to take me out to lunch at the Strand Palace; he was in the Canadian Mounties. He was tall and here on duty, very Canadian and had a tough wisdom about him, actually I think they might marry one day if the war spares them; they ought to be very happy.

Alec rang me to meet him at the top of Acacia Road at 10.30a.m., apparently we are going to Brighton, being Sunday.

I distinctly remember that awful day. Alec had passes to go to Brighton; some or most southern coastal towns were surrounded with barbed wire. MPs and some services were allowed to walk on the beaches and the Pier. For me, I felt sorry for poor old Brighton which has a reputation — regally, historically, some fine buildings, a wonderful theatre, and generations of population. We went to the Metropolitan Hotel for lunch, instead of having a good sandwich on the pier. All I could say to my mother was that the beach day was a complete and utter disaster.

March 1941:

My Dear M. I have not done very much except we have been working like buggery lately, several officers not reported or ill. Rimington was posted to Bristol last Wednesday. No one has taken her place yet, so Holmes goes up one and I've been helping her. This registration of women has increased enormously; people have rushed in all day. Wednesday night was very bad, homes and all buildings intensely bombed, but St Johns Wood escaped quite a bit. We still have every pane of glass in, although the noise was deafening and terrifying while it lasted, 9p.m. to 4a.m. I was out until 11p.m., about the only night I had elected to go out to dinner and be late. The morning brought our main streets looking like a hailstorm — covered with white glass, and buses were doing their best round back streets. Our unit (Victory House) was finally united about 12 noon.

I arrived not long after 8a.m., and a security officer asked me to go to the poor RAF C.O. who is elderly. He was in his pyjamas, he had lost every bit of uniform; he tried to keep calm, every brick of his house had gone; he was clutching a pair of flannel trousers, over his pyjama top he had a borrowed jacket. He was sitting at his desk, bewildered. You see, the London sky by 3.30a.m. was pure orange; the Germans kept returning singly with packets and dropping them on the fires. In the early evening I found that the sky sounded like an aerial motor factory. Kenneth's Royal Academy of Dramatic Art got a land-mine in the centre and he is completely shattered by it, having organised it from the foundation stones.

To return to the C.O. at the Air Ministry at Victory House, I seem to have given the C.O. aspirin and

162

organised the usual cup of tea. I was disturbed about his wife and family, but everyone had survived.

The following Saturday evening, Irene Vanbrugh invited me to the Q Theatre where she was playing "Viceroy Sarah"; it was the original cast who performed at Whitehall a long time ago. It was all about the Duke of Marlborough, and Irene took the part of Sarah. She was very good (she is 68 years) and performing twice a day including Sundays. Kenneth and I drove back with her and got in about 9p.m. (Remember it is hot, evening theatres had to begin about 5p.m. because of the raids.)

Then the second blitz began, the guns seemed more active and not so many bombs near us or fires, one could not go to bed with ease so Kenneth and I stayed up to midnight playing Triominoes, which is a fascinating game like triangular dominoes. Then in a lull I went to bed and fell asleep before the All Clear at 4a.m.

St. Paul's Cathedral on Fire

I hear St Paul's was still blazing up to 11a.m. London is looking very bedraggled, and yet you can still turn into a square or street which seems quite normal. Kingsway itself is remarkably free, only two craters and one bit of a house near Holborn in the whole street. On Thursday, restaurants had no gas or water, so we ate standard corned-beef, tinned potatoes, cold beans, beer and tinned fruit. Acacia Road has all its electric light, gas and water!

Dear M. Today, Sunday we went down to Kenley to have lunch with Barnes. The WAAF Officers have moved off the camp into a delightful large house with a glorious garden, three tennis courts and a swimming pool. The food for lunch was excellent, meat apparently is not short in the Service (here).

Rationing in wartime varied and the services had their rationing system. Rations for a ship, Navy ashore, RAF and the Army varied according to the work and sometimes occupation. The worst off were the civilians in towns and places where they could not garden or keep chickens, two pigs and rabbits. To assist, the outer parts of cities or even along the railway, vacant blocks and allotments were eagerly taken up and were sought after and jealously guarded. Many publications and leaflets of simple and nutritious meals were issued. The evacuees who had been sent away to small towns and villages were sometimes a problem, and often a great help. I think the big cities had the worst burden because of direct bombing on homes, warehouses, docks and convoys carrying supplies from overseas.

I quote from a letter in March:

Being in Air Ministry, I have full civilian rations, Lily the cook (St Johns Wood) being rather dull, and we, being in a full residential quarter, get no concession from the trades people. In poorer quarters the population cannot afford butter or meat, so the butchers sell their surplus stock to those customers who can (afford it) on their cards . . . The news is very serious and rather terrifying but one can only hope the Indian Army will get rushed over from the other side. If we can hold Africa and then swipe Italy, then we can work round Greece again if we lost her. The Van (War Weapons Base van with posters and pamphlets) has been cancelled so David will not be coming, Corporal Chapman will be coming with me by train. How we shall get about I don't know. Also we are only doing St Ives and Penzance. Since

165

then I've been told to take things quietly. I am coming down (to Cornwall) on the night train on Thurs. arriving Friday.

So from Thursday week until Sunday I shall be rather free, until then very busy. I have not decided which shops we can have in St Ives. I have written to Mr. Freeman, the Mayor, Mr. Drage, the Chamber of Commerce chairman, my friend, the Town Clerk of Penzance, and Nancy Williams — she is on all sorts of committees (an old friend). Tonight I came back (to St Johns Wood) by the normal bus route, the streets are all cleaned up now and only the actual craters are barricaded off. Everything is normal. It is very sad about Greece isn't it? Did you get the lb. of cheese I sent 14 days ago? I fear the postman may have eaten it en route?

I'm so sleepy I could sleep for weeks. After the two blitz nights, people are pouring into recruit.

Those two blitz nights I think could be the worst thing I have been through and will experience.

I seemed to be plodding through the recruiting still and the recruits, with a lot of homeless joining up; I knew I was in a dead end job. I could not get my promotion because sick leave in the past was deducted from your time. I dined with Margaret on Sunday 22 April and gave her 36 rounds of ammunition for her birthday!

Sheffield

11 May 1941:

Just a quick line. On my return from Harrogate last night I found out I'm now a Section Officer (S.O.) and being posted to Sheffield. I was so flabbergasted — all the way down in the train I thanked my lucky stars I was not in Yorkshire. I hate the country, with its black stones and black earth. Still Betty Llewellyn (the now retired WRAF who asked to make a film of me) is in Sheffield. A Group Officer, I like her though I shall not be working with her or near her, but she will be someone there that I know. I shall not be too far from Harrogate from the Pearces or Campbell-Wards or from Honor Capill. I am to aim to York so my Sq/Officer says to run my own show. Sheffield! Can you imagine such a spot? Margaret Sims has been reposted to Llandow — still in South Wales but very happy, which is something. She always has been in luck until now.

So a new life begins, I get 4/- a day extra. My promotion begins on 26 May to RAF Flying Officer. I expect I'll like it. I usually settle down anywhere. I will have police introductions too. Sergeants Cleator and Malcolm who were in West Drayton kitchens asked after you in Harrogate. Will write anon . . .

25th May, North East RAF Area HQ:

I have arrived among the knives and forks! Home. What a place, pouring with rain and everything is black and dreary. Flt/Officer Griffin is in charge and seems very kind. She told me of this billet — 30 Bristol Road, Dover Road, Sheffield 11 which is an ordinary road but quite near the botanical gardens. The houses and streets seem quite black with soot.

The C.O. (RAF) is an uncouth Yorkshireman with no manners at all. I have applied to go to York, which will be a little bit better than this, and I shall be alone. Although Victory House is the parent unit, everything is run differently and they do not observe our little ways of entering things up. I talked to Betty Llewellyn and she is ringing up Monday. She is away this weekend. I go to work at 9.30a.m. The M.O. (Medical Officer) is a nice Scot, but hates Sheffield in every way.

I received a hurried note from Irene (Vanburgh) in pencil:

Dear Daphne P. Thank you for your letter. You do not seem very gay, but I do hope things may shake down. I will be seeing you. I have written to Miss Ulyatt, Wilsic Hall, Doncaster, and Mrs. Gerald Stone, Springbank, Whanncliffe Side, Sheffield. I have given your address, so you may hear from them. Miss Ulyatt lives at Wilsic, it actually belongs to a nephew of hers who is of the Umbry Steels firm Rotherham and brother-in-law to Mrs. Gerald Steel. Ronald is not often at home. He was in the Light Anticraft, then was attached from that and sent to America on a special job probably to be in with Steel. He got back about three weeks ago. He has a nice, rather newly married wife. Anyway they are old, charming and very easy friends of mine. When I come up on 20 June I shall probably go for a week to Wilsic and we might have a gay little two days together. They are also special friends of Lee Unisuter Bradley who first introduced me to them. What a long screed. My love to you . . . Irene.

Dear mother, the ENSA lunch yesterday was a huge success. Made even more so by the first Lord of the Admiralty himself announcing "the sinking of the Bismarck". Apparently in 15 minutes you can get to the country. If fine I shall go on a bus to Dore and Totley and find a billet in a farm. On 14 June I return to Gerrads Cross via London, great joy, where for 14 days I have to swot at administration. I've nearly forgotten it all. By then I hope I shall have news of a posting, South or South West.

Whilst I've been writing, gosh, lightening and thunder, terrific cracks. Now the lightening has just burnt up a balloon. You'd think they would have proper conductors on and rubber pads.

Bulstrode Course

A letter postmarked Sheffield; 26 May, Monday (My birthday was on 26th):

My Dear M. Thank you so much for the scissors, just what I wanted as I do not possess a pair that cuts, let alone a pair that folds up. I simply hate Sheffield but it won't be for long. Sunday was a fearful day. I took a tram to their so-called country, so did everyone else! The moors were steep and black and grim. I walked five miles round and came back to a fire and a book. Monday I went to the theatre and saw an amazing play with our doctor, who is always in a perpetual state of gloom but is very nice. The play was very funny so we laughed a great deal. Then we went to a hotel and drank Horlicks, being my birthday.

Every minute I look forward to my course on 16 June, even if I have to sleep with five other officers and we have little or no bathing accommodation. Still Barnes passed and she can't even spell, although her drill is pretty good, and I may not be doing that. (Ironically, of my two best friends, Margaret's writing looks like Arabic in reverse and

Daphne B.'s is only just readable if you tune into phonetics!)

I shall be able to be up in London on Sundays anyway. I'd give anything to be top because so many officers think I became an officer because of the ribbon. Sheffield local papers made a great fuss of my arrival, which annoyed me — they have their daily and evening and few London papers seem to be sold. Isn't it marvellous about the Bismarck, but awful about the Crete losses. I hope you are keeping well and you have someone with you.

A letter written in June, the address was Sheffield billet, Saturday afternoon:

My Dear M. I have only another week and have discovered that most of the tests at this course are oral, which are awful. I felt more confident with written exams. I suppose it is to save time and paper. Another officer has reported for RAF Admin. duties, she also hates it here. Still she may be moved. I am spending tomorrow outside Sheffield at Wharncliffe Close, with some friends of Irene Vanbrugh. Tonight, I shall go to the Group Fitness to introduce Crawford before I go. Last night I went to the theatre, as I'd not been out in the week, it was "Batchelor Father", not bad, quite funny.

The Misses Wintle and Woolvine seem sorry I am going. I do not know whether to trail all my luggage down to London or not, as I am determined not to stay in Yorkshire. I hope I can get an effective posting somewhere else, even if it means giving up recruiting. I am not very happy about this Bulstrode business now.

I have to swot up on Gas, Fire, Medical, Messing, Air Ministry Orders, Uniforms, Ranks in the three Services, Drills, Station Administration, Station Defence, Discipline and Morale, Dependant or Ordinary Allowances, Communications and Pay, Service Etiquette, Documents, Correspondence and Equipment. If I can answer all those questions without writing or thought it would be a miracle.

Betty Poulson lives with her father at St Buryan. I see them when I can in Cornwall, they grow perfect asparagus and the most wonderful strawberries like they used to be. On their part of the cliffs is where Marconi laid his first cables. Their Cornish stone house is old and very comfortable. As a character Betty Poulson is very intelligent and independent, in a way that she becomes remote from everyone, but she is quite friendly and writes to me.

Clothes rationing is in, I don't expect it will affect you much. The workers in Sheffield get very high wages, they deserve it but they spend most of it on wireless sets.

I'm sorry Hugh Walpole has died. Kenneth said Geoffrey Tearle rushed down to Cornwall as soon as war was declared and did the same last war. He has just resigned from the committee of ENSA. I must remember to send you some ha'penny stamps. Have not a chance to go into a grocer to send you something extra to eat.

Postmarked 24 June Gerrards Cross:

"Well I've done it again," (*I wrote*.) "I have just got up and had to crash in the middle of the course with a high temperature. London told me to report to Guildford on Monday. I've been asked if I'd like to go to the sea, so I am going to Torquay for certain." (*I seemed to fail in health all the time*.)

Sheffield — a Tribute to the Steel Workers

In between the visits and the end of War Weapons Week, and after Irene Vanbrugh's kind introductions, I spent one week with the Steels at their home. I had a wonderful insight into the production of steel to its ultimate finish of steel bars that were transported to the factories.

From manager to foreman, I was led around and introduced to groups when they had pauses, also lunchtimes, just minutes only sometimes, to carry the message, "Thank you for your important work", stressing the use of steel for hangars, engines and ultimately bombs. I did feel very honoured to meet these men, with their strength of will to accomplish dangerously hot furnace stoking, the extraction of red-hot bars, and the steam cooling of the metal. I reached as many as I could and, when I returned at the end of the day, Gerald and his wife were able to fill in the gaps. It was an intensive, mind-boggling week. I wish I were able to write in more colourful detail what

I saw and felt, as I squatted down with them as they rested.

In hindsight, the grime, the sooty soils and blackish walls were the industry's mark on the countryside. Even if I had been a man and fit, I would not have stayed the course.

Cornwall — a New Home, H.M. Coastguard, Gurnards Head

Before I transferred to Torquay, I did some homework about getting hold of the evacuated Coastguard cottages. I went into the Ministry of Shipping, which I believe was a hive-off in the Admiralty. I dived in and asked to see the Senior Naval Officer in Charge. To my surprise I did not have to wait long, and was shown into a large office with an elderly Navy Captain sitting at his desk. I gave him my best salute and apologised for coming directly to the point; I asked if there was any objection to my mother and aunt occupying the Gurnard's Head Coastguard Station. At stated times, if required, they would man the Pilot's room, which had a telephone linked to the lookout on the Head. The Captain called in his offsider who made a call to Exeter, under which area Cornwall was. The reply was, "No objection." So afterwards I was given all the paperwork to do for Exeter, and later was told in writing that my mother and aunt could have the two houses.

I wrote to my mother on 1 July:

The Ministry of Shipping said the Coastguard was vacant — all communications now go to Exeter and there was no objection. I'm writing this in a hurry. The Ministry said I was to give them a poke, so we come under the RAF, so there is a complete change in all procedures.

My next thought is to find a billet in Torquay. Monday, I report to Bristol and stay with Margaret Chamberlain. Tuesday, Torquay recruiting centre.

Of course, one cannot live on views, but it is one of the wildest and most glorious cliff areas. The lane down begins at the local pub on the road, with a postbox and a scattering of cottages in that vicinity. The lane on the other side branched off to the Head itself, which is shaped like the fish with a humpy head. There was a covered well and an electric pump in the Pilot House pumped water into all three houses.

Torquay — RAF Recruiting

Torquay 1941:

My Dear M. I have had an awful time searching for a billet, most of England has descended on Torquay and people are sleeping on sofas in hotels even. The RAF officer was very decent, the airwomen's convalescent home and section officer had a partitioned bedroom which she let me share. So from there I searched and canvassed over 30 places. They are all full or cannot give me meals, and all spare rooms have been commandeered by the local hotels who are making pounds. However an old dame said the Vicar had seven airmen cadets billeted on him and they had gone. Of course it was sleeping only in their case and a curious role, for officers cannot force a civilian to feed them, only give them a bed.

I went to St James Vicarage, Upton Hill Road, Torquay, and Mrs. Lane, the Vicar's wife, who was very sweet and kind, asked me to come round the next day. Her husband who is 70 said "No" firmly, because they lived very simply and there was no food in the shop (mind you, I've never seen such food since the beginning of the war like those shops!) then in the next breath, he said, "Do you want to come tonight?" So I am in. Then at supper he said, "I'm glad you are here because of air raids and my wife must not be left alone, as I have to fire watch the church." Although actually if there is a raid of any size, I have to see to my own RAF building which has three stories and a basement.

It was difficult to get any idea of money from them. They insisted on giving me their daughter's room and I should just pay for food. So I make my bed and wash the supper things up at night and take the dog (dachshund) out for a stroll. The convalescent home is only 200 yards away and Witley, the S.O., is very kind and extremely nice; at present her husband is in the Gold Coast, both South Africans.

I've met Matron who is at the huge RAF hospital, two miles the other side of town, who has invited me to the RAF cinema and their own beach with every kind of game. She is the first matron I've met who is genuinely nice and human. There are various HQ and different units.

Rimington was at Bristol and Margaret met my crowded train and missed me, and had to rush back because she was on duty. I eventually traced her and she came out for two hours. I went back with Rimington for the night. Bristol did not expect me until Friday but my duty sheet said Wednesday 30th.

"Mournful" (I don't remember her real name) is at Melksham in Wilts, a truly awful camp but very good for experience and she is getting on very well. Apparently Webster works here until 7p.m. But I am going to shut our office around 5.30-6p.m. Also I shall have to do RAF recruiting as well, and arrange their medicals. Bristol said it will be a rest cure but it's a really big job.

Dear M. Of course I will send you a Sunday paper. We are frantically busy, through the RAF leaving everything in a mess. It will take ages to sort things out. I'm trying to get a parcel off today as on Monday and Tuesday there will be two medical boards on and they have called up all my people, who have been waiting some time. I have a very nice willing Corporal, Corporal McGoldrick whose father is at the Coastguard Station, St Ives. She goes on leave next Friday she is very shy but very efficient.

Wing Officer Forbes-Sempell is a patient in the hospital. I go up and see her, as she has had an operation on the spine. The Squadron Officer from HQ is coming to see me to discuss my future. This week we have broken this depot's records for numbers, and if all those I've written to turn up, I believe it will be the first depot in this area to succeed in getting their target."

1st September 1941:

I was relieved to get your letter. Corporal and I are carrying on alone. I found the Buckfast wine in the merchant's opposite. I'm having another attempt at Gloucester next week for the Trade Test Board, I get glued to interviews and the phone, I have a lot of men to see, which takes time to get them registered.

On 13 September Sir Henry Wood is coming down and Matron, Mrs. Lane, and I are going to the concert.

The doctor and I are seriously thinking of going to see "Valerie", a reputed clairvoyant and palmist, only we do not want to be seen in uniform. I have to give a lecture tonight on Gas or Aircraft recognition for 40 minutes. I find our lectures are very well attended, the place is full.

2nd September:

I am having a busy week next week as I may have to go to Gloucester. Then I hope to get 48 hours and come and see you on the 3.24p.m. train from Newton Abbot. I have one more free railway warrant which must be used. Can you put me up 30th-31st?

Torquay is simply packed with visitors, you'd not credit a war is on. Recruiting is going well. The Annual Inspection took place today and the Group Captain I.R. seemed very pleased with everything, the books and the condition of the place. We've really slaved to get it clean, I scrubbed the medical quarters several times. He was decent enough to say that the improvement to the depot was noticeable in the short space of time I'd been there and he was cheered to think a woman could run a depot by herself. He said I was to do masses of men's recruiting and was equal to any RAF officer with regard to enlistment and duties. I then had a nice letter wishing me good luck in my job and it seems I'm here for a while. Now about the parcels, I am sending you one every week because the Lanes refuse to take more money. They are doing it for the Service, for your and Daddy's sake, so the money is extra, as I can get any amount of food here.

Torquay, Military Hospital

Here we were again. I honestly thought the Gremlins were after me:

I got rather a cough and could hardly talk so stayed at the depot, as there were two children in the house. Also I did not know whether I'd have to go sick. The complications of being ill in a billet are difficult. I slept at the depot until they took me to hospital. I hope to be up soon. Webster, the Exeter RAF, has taken over the recruiting.

I have a wireless and matron comes twice a day with things. Mrs. Lane brought flowers out of the garden. If I get any leave after this, could Aunt Edith put up Grimley (Lorna); her fiancée was killed in Dunkirk and now her home has been blown up by a bomb in London. Her parents were saved and they are living in one room in London where her father has his business; but that part of London was blown up and he is 70 years old and he is opening up a new place. Grimley has not taken leave since she dashed up to help them. I feel rather guilty having been on her hands for several days until I was ignominiously removed by field ambulance. Grimley has just arrived to post this. As you know she was a fully trained nurse, never knew why she left. It was something to do with elderly parents.

A few days later I wrote:

Better today, taken me off that awful M&B 693. We are fully staffed with the Princess Mary's Nursing Service and VAD, men are nursing orderlies, and I have a male nurse at night and a sister. As you may know this really is a men's hospital, a number of smashed-up pilots are here.

It's all rather amusing as you know I smile crookedly, well, a neurologist said to me and matron that I'd got Bell's palsy. I was given electrical treatment and great fuss was made about pulling my face straight. Meanwhile I remarked I'd rather get my jaw right, and asked for the senior RAF dentist and we both insisted on pulling my top wisdom tooth out. I felt shattered and very odd, with a cough and congestion. Now they say my mouth is straight and they are very disappointed they've not got a case of B.P. to go on with.

Poor Grimley had a bad time as a Dr. Cawthorn (RAF) said I'd got pneumonia as well. I was oblivious to all this, I just knew I felt painfully ill and could not afford to be; but it was clear I would

185

not be out of this under five weeks. I am now reminded that my investiture takes place within five and a half weeks. If I'm to take two people I ought to ask Barnes, but she has so much in life and much social glamour that I feel Lorna (Grimley), who has nothing but bad luck, should go after what she has done for me. Margaret Sims is in South Wales, she has everything in life, too. What I suggest is that you write to the Thrings and see if they will put you up for a night or two and we could go to the theatre. I believe there are several good shows in London now. Alec wants us to meet, and Holmes and Margaret Sims may be in town but, although one is apt to take advantage in town, one must not get too involved. Then you could drop off at Reading to see Mrs. Brooke-Smith (a life-long friend of my mother).

I do not know whether I shall get seven days' sick leave or do all the convalescing here. This is actually a convalescing hospital, and out of the 150 patients here there are only 16 bed patients. Most men are recovering from crashes or awaiting their arms and legs to be taken out of plasters, etc.

Lorna has had no leave for 12 months, except for seven days when she was digging furniture out solidly and she has nowhere to go if she does take it. She looks dreadfully tired at times because the convalescent depot, with the type of girl she has now, is a fearful responsibility, so I know if she will come with me if I ask her. Hence my asking about the Gurnards Head pub. The alternative was to go to Cuckfield and shoot down rabbits, the country and air is beautiful. Though of course I'd prefer to come home. I realise about the paraffin and things and how impossible that is, unless I get 10 gallons from somewhere. It's surprising what I do get. An orange arrived last night. The children under six sell them to adults for twice the money, cute little beggars. I think the civilian hospitals should have the oranges.

On 7 October I received a letter from Cornwall, and I tried to answer a barrage of questions:

You know I've got bronchitis, though possibly catching whooping-cough, and everything has cleared up; it's a question of time to stop coughing. I know I will not be out before another four weeks. Mrs. Lane will put you up and I will see if I can get a railway warrant or half-fare voucher, and I'll put it through the orderly room. I have come off the lodging list and I'm automatically on the hospital strength. My promotion has been deferred again. I'm sad I keep losing. The C.O. has visited with three doctors. Apparently they are making a plate of some odd bacilli and they've found I am a border case of a new whooping-cough, so it's provided a new interest in the lab if nothing else.

I was told my half-sister Irene was staying with my Aunt Vera, but if I did meet her I was now to call her

Veronica, not Vera. I think I was a bit surprised that neither Irene nor Aunt had visited or written, or even phoned the hospital, as they live in Torquay, but I had learnt long ago not to expect things the normal way.

I wrote:

I knitted quite a bit of scarf in the night and I dropped several (stitches) and had to ring my bell for a VAD to rescue them by torchlight whilst I drank cocoa. No knitting in the darkness! The West Indies and the Pacific have a special program all night transmitted by the North American BBC, Stephen King-Hall, 4.15a.m. I've learnt through the Investiture that I shall be here another six weeks. I'm just reading "North West Passage" by Kenneth Roberts.

Another letter written the following week says:

I cannot get up until my temperature is normal and I'm not coughing so much. Now it's four weeks to go. I have been told Pilot Officer Finch has arrived from Plymouth to take over the depot, so the men take over again. I mentioned that I might like to stay in Torquay, although I disliked the town, and listed the friends I had made and who had been so kind to me. My life is rather like a shuttlecock, and I feel I want to settle in a cabbage patch, unless it is to do an outstanding job with plenty of imagination.

Flight Officer Burnett has been in chatting, she is an extraordinary girl, some would say she is pretty. She and her sister (S.O.) accompanied her father, an Air Vice-Marshal, to Australia on some diplomatic move and have just returned. She says the hospital downstairs is like a Geneva conference, more Poles than anything, all the Dominions, one Turk (later eight), two Indians with blue turbans with their uniforms, Belgian and French.

One of the padres is seeing me tonight. I can get you some chocolate: we are rationed a bar a day as well as free cigarettes but I am not allowed to smoke. I have three packets, a patient drew them. I'm eating a lot of honey sent to me by the Upton Harvest Festival. Never did I think I'd receive a Harvest Festival present. I am sorry your parcels will be erratic, as I cannot supervise things. I hope you are not too short. I have no view yet, just sky and tops of trees in a very small room. I was in a large room, then other patients came and I was moved. Lucky really, even Flight Officers and sisters have to share rooms, but it's my coughing in the night and often vomiting that keeps others awake. Eventually the doctor asked me if I was lonely and would like to be with someone. That's the last thing I'd want, to be with strangers, I need my privacy. I have the USA concerts at night on the air. I hear the seagulls but I still can't taste hardly a thing between salt and sugar.

Reporting to Victory House

Dear M. I'm afraid I have not very good news for you, that is why I think it's wise for you to come to Torquay this Monday. I've lost my job here, which is perhaps natural after being away so much, but I have been sent to the ends of the earth, to Scotland. I am to be an adjutant they say to the WAAF Officers Convalescent Depot; as there is not one, they must mean the airwomen's, i.e. Sibley's, depot. Sq. Officer Turner, who is now my group officer, asked me if I'd care to go to Scotland and I said emphatically no. But Sibley was very attached to me and, what with her ingenuity and Turner's concern to get me out of recruiting, they've landed me in an outlandish spot. If it's Sibley's place, then it is the Duke of Hamilton's home. It is miles from the nearest village, 20 miles from the town. Plenty of fishing. He (the Duke) was made to go there because he had a weak chest, so the combination of things proved too much.

Lorna is very upset, she brought me the news, her face was awful. I've written to the Postings Officer, to Victory House for reconsideration. Turner, you met her in town, thinks she's doing me a world of good. I'm quite shattered. Mrs. Lane came yesterday and her husband is very concerned, as he thinks I shall be posted soon. I suppose that's his Irish uncanniness.

Strange, that James should just be posted to Ireland. Lorna is finding out the cost of cars and buses. I suggest you stay from Monday to Saturday unless the Lanes ask you to stay longer, you are having my room. Lorna will bring you to the hospital, in peace days it was the Palace Hotel, and it's still like a hotel.

This war is sending me around alright, there is no mistake. I am waiting to hear from Campbell (Squadron Leader Med. Officer) when I can get up. I disgraced myself yesterday by being in bed all day coughing. I've been up Saturday, Sunday, Monday, one hour each day for tea and greatest of joys — a hot bath. I expect Lorna will meet you and take you up to the Vicarage. Torquay is now very large and is built into Paignton four miles away.

Pilot Officer Finch has arrived, he says Scotland is not definite. He's getting the C.O. to use his influence for the South. (I notice all these groups and command avoid the Medical Admin. altogether). I have just written to Margaret Sims from whom I've heard little.

I wrote to mother after her visit:

I'm glad you got back safely, sorry the train was late. Campbell has gone on leave. Everything is cleared up now. I'm having violet-ray treatment in the afternoon. I consider that's pampering. If the sun is out I can go out for half an hour. Cawthorn, the Depot doctor, has been posted very quickly. The new M.O. decided the inoculation doses have been too much. The medical orderly Johnston passed out for two days, the one whose hair you disapproved of!

The anemones are lovely and some are in bud. Campbell is back and says I must go out for 10 minutes and walk. I now may smoke, strange, when you can't you want to. (I was never a smoker, just joined in and put the cigarette out!) I hope you enjoyed your visit and are not too tired. We've had three nights of warnings although the BBC said there was no activity. I've had many letters from James prior to his posting to Northern Ireland, he wants to come here, I've said no, he has a lot to do at Cuckfield, he's neglected his house, his animals, the lake wants dredging.

The food is very good but I cannot taste a thing. I turned on the set as the announcer said here is Mr. Beechman (Alec), member for Penzance, his weekly talk on Westminster. He was good but very self-conscious. It's hard to talk to a box with everyone staring at you.

Investiture Change — B.E.M. for G.C.

Dear M. An RAF Officer has come to see me to say the Under-Secretary of State for Air says I will receive an invitation to attend Buckingham Palace shortly to receive the George Cross and be re-invested. Also I am to curtsey and not to salute. The latter has shattered me . . . in King's uniform! Can't they see how awful it is? The Empire Gallantry Medal has been superseded by the George Cross, which is a great honour, coming next to the Victoria Cross.

Would you please send my medal back — my ribbon will be blue now with a silver cross. The post-woman will register it."

My Dear M. It's marvellous getting such an early release. Campbell (S/Ldr M.O.) called me in and said "How are you, you're looking much better — do you feel fit to work again?" Then he said that, pending my medical board this Wednesday, I can have one week's sick leave. The Group Captain (C.O.) said Lorna could have hers at the same

193

time. We are both excited at coming down. Can you have us and is Lorna Ticehurst coming? We have already been collecting butter, tea, sugar and cooking fats on coupons. We will try to bring meat along but we cannot promise, as one cannot buy it overnight so to speak. I have rung up my ex-C.O. who says nothing can be done about my posting until the finding of the medical board, but he is willing to put forward the result to my Group Captain in London, if favourable, to claim me back.

Campbell said I am very fit and thinks the finding will be to go anywhere and do anything. Also it was definitely a whooping cough. If I'm fine I am going over to Teignmouth this afternoon. I have got a good colour and I'm very sun burnt in the bath with my violet-ray treatments.

Had tea with Mrs. Lane and she showed me your letter. Lorna gave her sugar and tea for you, and she was quite offended, so we are bringing it down.

A Squadron Leader RAF Medical Officer, who is very charming but has lost the nerves in her right arm and is in dreadful pain, is on my floor; she is nice and very clever. (One feels so helpless when you know somewhere in the world there is relief or a cure.) Thank you for The Cornishman, I passed it to McGoldrick. Will write Tuesday and wire next Wednesday. My Board may be in the afternoon.

RAF Uxbridge

Thurlow House, Torquay.

My Dear M. I rang up and found you had gone to breakfast. The next day I spent listening to all the arguments put by Air Ministry as to where I should be posted. I'm quite shattered as they said I was so overdue for S.O and the only vacancy they had was in Lanarkshire and, unless I wished to be in the South West as an A.S.O. indefinitely, I had to choose. They refuse to allow me to go back to recruiting for health reasons, as I was so overdue for promotion I had no option but to go to No. 2 Convalescent Depot, Strathavon, Lanarkshire. Everyone is so convinced that it will be the making of my health. Squadron Officer Turner says its madness for me to go to Scotland; she has now offered me a Photographic Training job in Blackpool. As I await these days I am to report on the fifth to M.T. Training School, RAF Station, Morecombe, Lancs. What I'll have to do with transport etc. is beyond me. Morecombe faces the North Atlantic and is the coldest spot in England. Tonight I'm going out with Squadron

Leader Roué, a Chaplain, and then I'll see the Lanes for a fleeting visit. I'll report back to London tomorrow. Under separate cover I've sent a parcel.

I went up to London to report to RAF Station, WAAF Hospital, Uxbridge; one had to be cleared or re-cleared medically as Recruiting came under Victory House, Kingsway. I found everything rather vague; I was to attend lectures on administration. I had hardly begun when I ran the usual temperature so I missed one week, but I did not do too badly. I came 10th out of 22; Class A was 80%, B over 70%, C under; I got 69 marks. Five minutes more swotting would have done it.

The Nursing Sisters were very kind. At the convalescent stage, both men and women were together. Poles, Australians, Canadians and Czechs.

I returned to the fold of the camp which was huge. One side contained an Army regiment, and in the centre was a very large parade ground. I felt thrown back to the raw realities. Quarters were very overcrowded. I had to sleep with another woman called Pine in a hut with bunks. She was rather new and I believe had a refresher course and then was on the administrative staff with me. Uxbridge was a very confusing area: we were not in the centre of the town, but just outside. The train service was good. The hospital was quite extensive and there was a separate part for women, near the officers' married quarters, which were quite nice homes with gardens facing the lovely park where the Duke and Duchess of Kent resided.

To my great joy Barnes was on leave two miles away from London; she told me she had been made Squadron Officer and to her horror posted to Gloucester — a far cry from her set-up at Kenley amongst the fighter Squadrons with quick access to London. James was still in Ireland and near Londonderry; he had been admitted into the Londonderry Military Hospital, what with I could not imagine except that he got bad chills so easily.

The news at that time could not be worse and I felt I should never be alive to see the end of it. China had been fighting for four years and things there could not improve. America would have to come to terms with realities and come in with real vigour, if she did not want huge initial losses.

I gathered through my Flight Officer that my extra ring had to be approved by this C.O.; as she was very popular with the RAF I hoped she would expedite things.

By this time my mother and aunt had really settled in the coastguard station and were exploring, adjusting to a new routine. I did not worry my mother, but I began feeling off colour and began to croak and I think I had laryngitis. Anyway, I reported sick and was admitted to hospital with a high temperature. I lost my sore throat and chill, but my temperature would not go down. I still felt very tired, depressed and off. The Senior Medical Officer was a Wing Commander, a very kind and unusual man; he and his wife were very musical.

He transferred me as a guest patient to his quarters, one of the nice houses opposite the Park. I got up in leisurely style in the morning; someone took my temperature night and morning. From the quarters I walked down a pleasant road to the boundary fence. One Saturday morning, I watched a man walking from the far side of the Park to a large pile of stacked up wood like a bonfire, right in the middle of the open park. He bent down and picked up an axe and for over an hour he chopped up everything into a neat pile of logs. He walked back to the wood or sheltering that surrounded the large house. Next Friday afternoon another load of wood appeared. The man appeared again, slim, average height, then it dawned on me it was the Duke of Kent taking exercise and getting away from it all.

Hospitalised — Ireland on Sick Leave

My host then said on Monday, "We want you in the hospital." I am sending you away for one month, everything has been approved of. Go up Wednesday to London, buy the bare civilian necessities. Where can you stay the night?" I said, "St Johns Wood." Daphne Barnes was up and I hoped I could go and see her. I was to travel in uniform, to Stranraer, stay the night at an address near the ferry, board the boat and cross to Larne, Northern Ireland. My job was to pick up a small case and never leave it about; there was a chain and padlock if I slept on the boat or train. I was to be a courier and take it to Londonderry. Train from Larne, Belfast. At an RAF Depot or Station I was to hand the case over as directed and be taken to the address given, which was Mrs. Stevenson, Knockan Bridge, Feeney, Londonderry.

So I told him how wonderful it had been to read and rest in his house with his family. I enjoyed the peace, the security with no responsibility. Also for a long time the Luftwaffe had let us alone here, although the fighting was bitter across the Channel. I went to the Orderly Room and collected my ticket — Uxbridge to Londonderry return via London — collected my ration book and was to call at Adastral House to pick up my brief case and a letter on the way to Kings Cross St Pancras.

I arrived in St Johns Wood and found Daphne B. there with her brother, Sir Ferguson Graham: he was a very serious edition of Daphne B. Then Kenneth arrived. I managed to get to Airtex in Regent Street, where I bought a royal blue and an orange shirt. I thought I would wear the colour suited to the Irish accordingly. Everything was done with great fun and I think we dined out. We must have celebrated Daphne B.'s new ring. Next morning I reported to the Inspector of Recruiting and was given another ticket: Derry to Penzance, Penzance to B. (HQ) for T., the place I was originally going to.

At Stranraer, there was almost a full-force gale blowing. I stayed the night, a very comfortable billet, and had a good breakfast on board. The ferry was very full with a regiment of soldiers, who were already looking very sorry for themselves. We were delayed some time. I locked my cabin up and was very intrigued with the briefcase. I changed into my battle dress, which seemed to be useful if we had any climbing to do; by the time we sailed it was night. At dawn I asked the purser if I could go on deck, he gave me a very funny look and said, "You'd be the only one", and gave me a lifeline. I staggered along towards the bridge and the Captain said, "Look, look," and northward was a school of whales spouting water in great arcs. The Captain said, "It's rare to see that, but the gale has forced them in." Later, he said, "There's not a soldier in sight. I'm surprised you've survived." At Larne someone, a RAF Red-cap (nickname for a RAF policeman) met me and put me on the one and only Londonderry train. I saw nothing of Belfast, south of Larne: I travelled alone, first class, and got some sleep, but the view of the country was lovely. I reported to the RAF at Derry and so I finished being a courier. It was not far to Knockan Bridge, an old, very big farmhouse; transport was provided.

The mountains in the distance were very beautiful, they were farmed for peat; at their base were luxurious woods, the air was moist and cloudy. All the food there was home produced, there were two other paying guests and relations. I was not allowed to wear uniform but fortunately I had my coat, a skirt, a pair of corduroy slacks, blue and wine-coloured pigskin shoes, and a royal blue pullover. I got everything in England by signing for it, no coupons, everything had been reduced due to rationing. The war was non-existent, we were just on the border, so that you could walk into Eire and at the end we were in Ireland.

I wrote to my mother:

The Stevensons have several thousands of acres including one of the three mountains called Paul. This first Sunday, a lot of police are on duty and they come in their black uniforms, walk in and up

201

to the piano and play a tune and everyone sings. Colonel Stevenson is now playing hymns. We go to the Church of Ireland at 9.30a.m. for a short service and we then have a light meal at 11.30, and high tea at 3.30p.m.

In the early morning everyone is up between 5.30 and 6a.m. with mock battles for defence practice. The newspapers come two days old. It is much colder here and without uniform its chilly, but we have huge peat fires; I think of the heat in the hospital, Uxbridge, perhaps it kept my temperature up. I am pretty sure when I return I will be taken out of recruiting.

In the early morning on weekdays I took a rod out and cast into quite a lovely steadily running stream behind the house. Soon in my basket I had a lovely lot of brown trout, all caught on worms. There were stones set flat on the water, so I was able to clean them all for breakfast.

It was a standard stone-built house, with the front entrance almost in the centre and a nice wide hall to hang the many coats and hats. On the left was a very large dining room which seated 20 plus for Sunday breakfasts, with a very large sideboard. Standard offerings were porridge, plates of bread and butter, a large loaf on a bread board, one meat dish of lamb chops, another of fried trout, and a dish of eggs. At the far end was a vast kitchen. The owners had a good supply of help, men and women. The main market events discussed were about the stacks of peat cut and the quality and future dates of cutting. There were plenty of sheep with coarse wool, but at that time they were only of use for food. The stables were well away from the house. Talk was also about the quality of the distilleries; there seemed endless ones, quite illegal, they seemed to change their areas according to the purity and taste of peaty waters.

I felt there was so much to learn but it was hard to keep up physically. We had one day strolling down Londonderry's main street when I noticed the shops were well stocked. Liquor was very under-priced compared with England. The radio was turned on in the evening, but there was little or no discussion about the war. However, one of the male guests and a couple of police said it was unbelievable: we could go over the border and meet a relative or friend, drive down to Dublin and in any hotel or pub meet Germans and have friendly discussions and learn a lot. There were the minor diplomats of non-allied countries having dinner together. It was the craziest world I had met and if I had not been there I would never have believed it.

James Floyd's unit was near and he came over and fished and spent one weekend, but he was not allowed to be in mufti and sometimes this was awkward. I took some nice informal snapshots. I did not write much to Cornwall, as I knew my mother and aunt would not understand my suddenly being in a strange place. I was there for the Remembrance of the Battle of the Boyne; I think it was regarded as a national day. The Stevensons were incredible raconteurs. They were elderly and felt their offer to the RAF was a kind of help for rehabilitation, as well as being in very good circumstances. I was alone with the Colonel when we went up the mountain one morning and was carefully shown how to cut peat, the length of stacking. There were three to five men there at certain times, staying in the cottage, or cottages, Monday to Friday for the season. Nobody rushed or hurried.

I wrote to my mother that I was sailing on 17 March to London to report, collect my ration card and go to St Ives or Penzance. I would have 14 days' leave left. That is my sketchy story of Knockan, Feeney. Time will never dim those lovely colours and rich Irish songs and dreamy mountains.

London to Penzance — Sick Leave, to RAF Victory House

I went home and then back to Uxbridge. Wing Officer Turner (originally of Kent) had never seen me so well and she asked after my mother. I felt I must start packing my things in case I got little notice, or got to a camp where there was a scarcity of water, as clothes must be washed and ironed. The heat was terrific, the men were allowed to take their jackets off, but not women. I washed my hair quickly, and my shirts around the cuffs and the collars.

I was longing to be posted from Uxbridge — I hated it as much as ever.

I arrived back to much illness and to many changes, which is rather disconcerting. All our officers are moved to the main camp much further from the Mess and near a busy road; the quarters are small and very dirty. S.O. Pine has lost her voice and is very ill. No one seems to have done anything. S.O. Harmon-Morgan seems to think she was swinging it, but when I saw her I thought she was nervously exhausted, and very ill with a bad chill. So I went to the hospital and got her admitted.

Causton has a bad cold and has scabies and looks rotten. Harmon-Morgan herself can hardly speak and conked out with a bad chill and sickness at lunchtime.

I cannot move for filth, so I have commandeered three airmen and a RAF Corporal to scrub the walls and floors of Administration tomorrow at 8.30a.m. The C.O. was very nice to me this afternoon.

All this need not have happened if, in the order movement, someone had ordered a clean up. It was no wonder everyone was sick.

Earlier I mentioned the huge-sized parade ground. The area took four plus large units on Sunday mornings and compulsory parades; when all were assembled, there was a vacant large space in the centre of the square. The WAAF were usually on the left of the RAF Headquarters airmen. We faced the Army unit and on the left there was another RAF unit. One sunny morning, I was in charge of the WAAF unit, and unconsciously (to me) had slightly tipped my cap over to the left. I gave the usual parade drill to bring the WAAF up and marched forward to snap out to the Wing Commander (Administration ex-World War I) "Ready for inspection Sir", saluting. This officer always disliked me and I had begun to dread coming up against him at any time. To my amazement and disbelief, he roared at me from a few feet so that even the Army could hear right over the other side, "Pearson, you are improperly dressed, straighten your cap dead centre." I took two steps back, as I did, I firmly acknowledged the command with the naval acknowledgement "Aye, aye, Sir," straightened my cap possibly half an inch, stepped forward two paces and gave a stiff salute. I could hear stifled laughter and titters from some of the men, with N.C.O.s barking at them. It was never done to reprimand an officer without using a rank or to do so in front of personnel.

When the parade and service was over, we usually dispelled to our messes. When I got to ours. The WAAF C.O. said, "An invitation has come to have a drink in the RAF Officers' Mess before lunch, invitation excluding Section Officer Pearson." If I remember rightly only the minimum number went. Our nice C.O. the Groupie (the nickname for Group Captains) was away on duty that Sunday, so the Winco (Wing Commander) was in charge.

We had to work more than ever in the Service, and all I cared about was to go to bed soon after 9p.m., clean buttons and clothes and myself, in time to read a good book. Every third night now one was a duty officer, and with luck turned in at midnight.

Posted North, RAF Snaith

I was posted to Snaith, Yorkshire. I told my mother after I actually got there, because there were so many alterations and cancellations.

The mess here seems to be extremely happy, but several officers have been posted and there are only four WAAF officers. David, my RAF C.O., lets me fly, strictly speaking only on duty, but I could fly anywhere except on operations.

To explain: we had two satellite stations and cross-country runs, meaning the bombers repaired or serviced had to have daylight runs to test them out thoroughly, and fit in with personnel on duty, who had to go somewhere else from A to Z within the range of the aircraft tests.

It was a large new airfield south of Lincolnshire and being night bombers, and I suppose with the idea of German raiders coming in with returning aircraft, the authorities scattered the living quarters, which certainly would avoid casualties if bombed, but for daily work it was very awkward. The future WAAF Officer quarters were being built in the area by the Works Section with the WAAF airwomen already there. When I arrived it was very wet and the buildings were only half up, we never seemed dry — there was mud everywhere. There were two Code or Cipher Officers who were housed near the main RAF mess where we all had meals together. The ante-room was newly furnished and the mess was very near the administration offices, which was convenient.

The RAF Admin. Wing Commander has lent me his big bloodhound when I go down to the site on my rounds. One way to exercise him, a very obedient and loveable dog.

The C.O. Group Captain Thomson (David) has lived in Iraq for years and is rather lost amongst masses of people and gets bemused. We flew the other day, I took over for one hour, then David took control and did some inverted flying and hanging upside down, I nearly lost my helmet. I have been given a battle dress, which fits me like a glove, goggles and a helmet. A new WAAF Officer arrived, which helps me. David and I were asked to a wedding breakfast by the C.O. of a neighbouring station, as one of his Corporals is marrying one of our WAAF; it all went off very well.

I have been granted a permit to drive RAF vehicles and I can drive the Vauxhall, the C.O.'s staff car, when he is not using it. Lorna Grimley is still up north in Scotland and says she is much happier now her F.O. is away.

I have heard today that Air Ministry, via Oliver Daws, a jolly nice person whom I met at Harrogate, has approved of my staying here; also the Group Officer has conducted a detailed tour from 10a.m. to 6p.m., and seemed satisfied with the various changes. It is hard when so much is half built and everyone is new here to the service.

It may seem strange that we had been established now for several years and weren't settled in, but casualties, new trades and overseas posting for the WAAF caused waves of newly trained women. Official figures say on 3rd September 1939 we began with 1,734 WAAF, which included 234 officers. In 1943, on 1 October, we had the highest number of 180,339 WAAF including 53,179 officers; thereafter the numbers declined by attrition. When I left in 1946 (January) there were 4,373 officers. Also the occupation of Germany absorbed a lot of people and took much organisation.

The new personnel were posted to an unknown place, Snaith, without shops, creature comforts or homes, however humble, vast spaces, big bombers like giant bats, and a uniform code of behaviour which in their ignorance they thought they left behind on their course training.

I had to organise sports with other units from an army camp was not far away. I took over teams for two games of netball with ATS, I do not remember the results but it was fine. In the introductions I met a Colonel Gething, who took me later on to two other aerodromes in regard to defence. You see, we were so near the coast, yet whilst at Snaith I never saw the sea. After, we were shown the method of making trenches which is a technique for sand, being a very unsafe material. The following week we were getting some automatic .45 ammunition for practice, but I would not be allowed to rest the gun on my arm, so it would be out for the normal range. I began on 25 yards, which was nearer than our old Hitler target.

I also had a letter from Uxbridge, which was in an unhappy mess, also a note from my old Flight Officer, who was still livid at me for going on an attachment. So I was well rid of that unbearable place.

Joan Payne, the senior Cipher Officer, has been very kind and said I could go down to her office at night: it is very interesting there, and at times rather sad. The Squadron Leader who took me on a flight early on is missing. The Catering Officer who remembers me at West Drayton obtained her commission and has been posted here.

I was able to fly to Scotland and land at the hospital where Lorna was; she seemed very run down and was in bed.

All letters were censored in and out of camps now. It was very difficult getting to a Post Office but I tried to send my mother a parcel every week.

211

We had two satellites at Snaith — small stations operational for signals and radar. Generally there was one WAAF officer and two NCOs, and about 20 or 30 WAAF. That was why on the parent station we had a flow of officers being changed. You could not leave one officer alone for long, she was either relieved or replaced, and the same with the airwomen. There were airmen there hauling things about, usually under a senior RAF NCO.

To add to my duties I am in charge of gardening. Everything is pure sand and nothing grows easily. This is sugar-beet country. It seems to thrive here. So far I have been able to fertilise a large area near the Sergeants' Mess, putting in late-sprouting broccoli and cabbages. More land seems to be added. When I am not on evening duty I go down to the WAAF Quarters and the two NCOs, Flight Sergeant and Sergeant make me welcome and share their ante-room and mess with a lovely fire. My sleeping quarters are in a hut across the way with eight empty single officers' rooms!

In the middle of all this I was told to go to London for my medical board. Squadron Leader Campbell, the neurologist from Torquay, was there. He experienced the horror of the bomb attack the night after I left. He lost all his kit and equipment. Cordell-Bell, the pretty New Zealand VAD we called Tinker Bell, was killed, and all the patients were killed in the tower when they blew up our turreted rooms on all floors. Matron and Campbell were out and escaped at the time. I escaped certain death by 18 hours, having gone home.

I do not remember what happened at the Medical Centre. At Snaith, all I know was I left the Catering Officer in charge of the WAAF — I knew David the C.O. was to be posted.

I must have stayed overnight in town, probably at the Club, but as I was leaving I met Mr. Grimley outside the Berners Hotel and he took me to the Holyrood Arms for lunch. Later Mr. Grimley caught the train to Reading, where they were living. I knew I was to face a different Snaith when I got back, so I rang the Duty Officer or someone to say I would like to stay the night in town; that was all right, so I went to see *Flare Path* at the Apollo, then later *In Which We Serve*, with Noel Coward taking the Captain's part; it was the best film I had seen so far.

Upon my return I found many changes in the service; things happened so quickly. David came down to the Mess and drank a farewell glass. This was in the WAAF quarters as Jean, the Sergeant, and Vera, the Flight, could not go into the RAF Mess. He raised his glass to Jean, calling her Bricks; she was a good brick in character and also had the habit of tidying up the odd bricks lying around. He called me Bruiser, because I walked into a wall and had blood streaking down my nose. So I got teased and asked "How is the black-out?"

Extracts of letters sent to my mother in Cornwall:

We now have Group Captain Gray — enough said. He is very strict — parades, etc., so we all keep away as much as we can. Tonight, an Air Ministry official invited us to a pub where he was staying, then on to a station dance for one hour.

I find I have been given an airman, son of a farmer from Dorset, to help. I have been trying to find a tractor to borrow or hire. Also, Evans from South Wales, an ex-commercial traveller. So I put him on to making paths with ashes, cement and brickwork, then we made a small drive in for cars and parking, and a sheltered lawn to sit or lie on. I have been given another five men and 23 acres, and a local farmer lent me his tractor which we had to thoroughly overhaul. We shall have many disappointments because we have millions of army grubs in the soil, which will eventually turn into hordes of caterpillars. Air Ministry heard of all this and sent me an Agricultural Advisor who covered our area and was most helpful. Another department arrived to build something on a horrible site which was an old river bed of the Trent and Humber, most of it was pure sand, so I was glad to lose that area.

I was sitting in the sun in our new garden on Sunday. I had taken the morning off. A new officer, recently arrived on attachment to relieve me, connived with the cook for me to have breakfast in bed! Anyhow S.O. Long is invaluable, how she got into the service I cannot imagine. She had been a state registered nurse for 18 years, reliable, excellent at organising, miles older than me. I thought she would be good at counselling the airwomen.

There are some queer war diseases about. I have got Trench Mouth. Scabies have begun again, so Long and I pounce on suspected victims and they are cured in 48 hours.

My aunt and my mother, were a curious combination of characters — Aunt Edith was tall and in age, rather gaunt. She had been in the Land Army in World War I. She enjoyed the work and made quite a few friends. She was physically strong. I think she enjoyed being of use and was a great help with most of the people I sent down as recuperating paying guests. The greatest asset for them was that anybody with a personal loss did not have to meet people or be gushed over. We fixed the minimum board and lodging, so it helped everyone with an extra ration card, especially a service card. The coastguard houses had one twin-bedroom and a rear room; Edith made hers into a bed-sitting room. On the ground floor was a laundry at the back, and an inside lavatory and bath. In front was a long room facing the sea, the far side with living or sitting area, the part near the opening door had ample room to seat six people for eating.

The Pilot's room's entrance was adjacent to the dining area of mother's house, so the bell for the telephone was extra loud and could be heard by both houses. There was a sloping shoulder-height desk on which ordinance maps and Imperial sized sheets could be drawn on, to plot the ships' distances. Instruction books were vaguely wandering along the shelves. Everything was dusty when the two sisters moved in, but very clean underneath.

I managed, after much reasoning with the powers-that-be, that I should receive a dependent's allowance for my mother and just a small remittance to cover the work of messages sent to the look-out on the head, also sightings of ships and aircraft, because we could see part of the coast hidden by the coastguard. I even filled up a single RAF Officer's application form. It caused a bit of a fluster but there were a lot of WAAF Officers without private income supporting or aiding their next of kin, and I was well supported morally over this.

Viv (another WAAF at Snaith) was already visiting the NAAFI (Navy, Army and Air Force Institute) manager and making up a food or goody parcel for Cornwall; of course I paid for everything. The Orderly room was making out compassionate leave passes and railway warrants and so on. Our boiler man on the site had given me some real blue sweet-pea seeds for next year for Cornwall.

In depots, large stations (Snaith was huge in size) and service colleges and instructing areas, there was always a Church of England chaplain, and correspond-ing Jewish and Roman Catholic Priests, the latter not usually resident. The Chaplain usually co-operated with the C.O. over RAF bereavements, and with me if the man was involved with a WAAF. When it came to WAAF bereavements, I was usually left to do the counselling and worst of all, give the news of death. Each Station Commander, always RAF then, had his own rules.

What we took for granted then was that a great proportion of RAF worked at night on Night Bomber stations. So the WAAF, cooks particularly, had to have a night shift. This period was a great proving time for women. Old-fashioned courtesies, although much appreciated, never quite made up for our already skilled WAAF tradeswomen. Straight from modern practical courses, they were not treated as equals in many trades. In the 1942 period, the German attacks and the constant bombing of British cities meant that a lot of unproven RAF and WAAF city-born personnel had a rude shock when they were posted to outback stations. I think they were the most homesick.

When the weather was better and evening's light, Jean Stones found two bikes she could officially borrow, so we sped out of camp crossing over the Ouse and south along its banks. There were canals or dykes to relieve floodwaters. The evening sky reflecting in the waters was a Dutchman's delight. The roads were flat and soon we reached an inn; we sat outside with a beer. That is where I met the farmer who lent us the tractor. Later the locals were very curious, which is natural, as we had taken a lot of their land. On the other hand, the men had been called up and strangers had been put into the farms. A large farmer came and had a few words, and gave me a lot of information. He had heard that a woman was in charge of gardens. I said to him, "I'm thankful we are not to grow beet." I said I did not expect too much from our cabbages and sprouting broccoli. He told us how the water flow was managed. Of course in adjacent Lincolnshire, the soil is richer and heavy, hence the bulb and potato growing.

I was due for leave, but also due for a conference so I would have to get my leave in after that. There was another inspection by Wing Officer Forbes-Sempell, whom I knew at West Drayton and as a patient at Torquay, so that was encouraging. A Dornier 217 came in with a returning bomber squadron overnight, it was demolished and I have a cherished souvenir.

I returned to the pub called "The Ship" on the Ouse, still owned by Joseph Spetch and his forefathers for 400 years, with two cottages and one farm, the only buildings for two miles and all communication was by the river. The older men played dominoes; the wives knitted and drank stout. They met there like a family, every evening; Vera and one other took on the younger men at darts, both were good.

The Wraiths, our farmers, now used to me, lapsed back into full Yorkshire; he is taking us to market on Thursday where he was selling cows and heifers. He kindly drove us back to camp. I explained we had no civvies for the market and we were the only ones in uniforms. His farm is two miles from Drax and not far from where the

Derwent joins it. The sugar beet goes up to Selby and returns to Hull with sugar in the barges.

We are getting fresh eggs and fresh butter. The civilian stoker gave me a hare. James sent me £5/-/-. I forgot to tell you, last May/June there was a great area of uncut grass, and just at the time of budding we borrowed old and new implements, the WAAF (all volunteers) cut, raked up and then stacked the hay, it took several days and nights. Overnight someone came over the wire and swiped the lot. Everyone blamed the locals, but I am sure it was an inside job for a friend to sell. Having made ourselves known, I do not think our recent friends would do that.

Much later on, our staff melted away on courses, as always when we had a good deal of sickness. One Saturday, a member of the mess who was there on temporary duty, Viv Parry, was killed, which saddened us. Luckily I was up in the RAF Mess at 6.30a.m. and was called. My Administrative Officer was practically engaged to him, poor girl, naturally she was stunned. I hardly knew how to break the news to her.

The Germans were getting cheeky, buzzing in, or flashing in, to take the men working on machines in hangars by surprise. But our defence units were good. The *Daily Mirror* stated that the enemy came over Yorkshire; they certainly did, but no one was killed.

It must be understood that, although the camp was manned 24 hours a day, those like myself who could never go home on rostered Sundays off, usually rested or took short walks near the camp. The Officer shortage was so chronic that being Duty Officer so often was a very tied work day. All meals were inspected — a short visit in the kitchen, then along the dining tables. It gave a chance for anyone to complain. One watched the cooks handing out the food to the men and women in line. At night, I was semi-dressed if resting, otherwise patrolling round the camp where WAAF were working, relieving the RAF Duty Officer if required. Action at night began just prior to the planes returning from their missions. Sick quarters were away from the main offices — I had little to do with them at Snaith — except any sick airwomen were visited daily. Cipher Officers and Catering Officers were never Duty Officers because of their work.

It was Christmas; business as usual except that all the messes were voluntarily decorated. Leave was granted sparingly to the family man or anyone with illness at home. There was no chivalry in this war; the Germans by now were conquerors on paper but not in fact. Actually, I had not been under fire on Christmas Day yet. The ritual was followed; officers were invited to the Sergeants' Mess one hour before lunch, after short services held on the station in the open.

Officers then served the airmen their Christmas dinner. We then returned to ours in the mess. But the skeleton operational people did not drink. I may be wrong but I do not think Ops were deliberately planned for Christmas Day. I think I managed to get home three times out of six to Cornwall. It was a long, long way.

Windermere

The month after Christmas I went to York and stayed at the Hotel Embassy; I quote from a letter to my mother from there:

> I am attached to RAF Windermere on Wednesday for a whole month and shall not know whether I will return to Snaith. I am here in York to buy shoes, collars etc. as I am quite out. It is bitterly cold.
>
> I dread to think what Snaith will be like — not one Admin. Officer left.
>
> I did fly up to Scotland as Lorna was so full of misery. It was bad enough for us: the tank sprang a leak and we were out a long way from the coast. We landed and the plane was re-fitted, but we had to return as soon as it was done. Lorna had upset her father, she was in bed with a chill and annoyed I had not phoned, and did not even order lunch. I explained Snaith had phoned and could not get through. So I said goodbye and was very hurt. I went to her Flight Officer, who said she was behaving very oddly. She also said she disliked planes, so she never got her ring. I told her she

221

would be better to get married and settle down. My flight was ready and the weather was bad, so we shot back to Snaith.

Before I left, I was asked to get the runway cleared of light snow, so somehow I got 100 brooms, 100 WAAF including myself, and in sections we swept and swept the runway. The Met. people had forecast a sharp cold snap and we had to keep the runway ice-free for that evening. We were very tired but we were thanked. Now I have had my medical for the course — I may not do P.T. but I can have a shot at the drill if I wish. Will send address later. D.

I packed all my bits and pieces up in case I was posted after Windermere, the WAAF Instruction School for Senior Officers. I was at Belsfield Hotel, Windermere, Westmoreland, for one month. It was a lovely place but very wet. I knew a lot of people from West Drayton who had done well. I was very glad to have seen Butler-Jones who coped with me at Harrogate, sending me to hospital. I had brought with me several introductions to residents, but I did not want to go out at night, being so wet and dark.

The village was amazing; some London shops had opened up because of the school. Another course was due in the week following my arrival. The food was very good, better than Snaith, where my staff were very upset at my going. Vera and Jean wrote to say a real shocker had taken my place, who seemed to concentrate on giving parties and did not seem to care. Meanwhile I was bored stiff with the course.

I said to my mother in a letter:

I am writing this in recession time because I cannot concentrate on swotting up the most idiotic things imaginable. I wrote a thesis for three hours, which is about the only work I've done here. The climate does not suit me and I either feel sick or have a headache. Lorna Grimley is here and very unhappy and spends every other day in bed. The doctor says she may have jaundice or something else. She is a shocking yellow-brown — she is going home for 14 days' leave and has received a posting from this course to Debden in Essex. She can get home easily on her 48 hours off.

By then there were many courses going on and the noise before meals was simply appalling.

Have found a very nice inn behind the church with a lovely fire, no WAAF. I often go there at lunch times and in the evenings. We spend an awful time discussing, debating and talking with no purpose at all. We seem to be wasting the government's money in a shocking way. I have bought a lot of things for this course: gloves, two pairs of shoes, new stockings, ties and shirts, so I ought to be all right for another year. We are going to be issued with 80 coupons next May and not 100, and some will be stamped "C" so we can purchase certain civilian clothes.

Jean Stones, my Snaith sergeant, is getting married the Saturday after I get back, so I can go to the wedding. Her parents still seem to be very wealthy; they have a lot of property and seven cars, but Jean, in spite of it all, is very unspoilt and is a dear, but very independent and has a total disregard for any authority. She does not like, and failed, the OCTU because of that. The C.O. here says she cannot guarantee to send her to me if I put her up for the OCTU again to be trained.

The station (Snaith) rang me up to say that the Group Captain is away for seven days, so I dread the chaos when I return. The civilian boiler man has sent me a box of eggs. I had a fit when I saw them. I gave the C.O. here two anonymously and she thanked me; I said, "How do you know it's me?" She laughed and said, "It is all over the school that you receive eggs." Those and fresh milk are the items lacking in this war. I am reading Berlin Diary by W. Shirez, but I don't get much peace to read — there is time, no peace.

I began to feel rather ill and reported sick. I had a temperature and could not keep my food down. I was sharing a room with three others, we all had dysentery. We had hard tack (large, hard biscuits), apples, milkless tea and 2 oz of brandy per day; the latter has to be signed for on our mess bill. I had a letter from Jean and

Vera who said the C.O. at Snaith was very angry with my replacement whom I will not name.

I was discharged from sick quarters feeling rather wobbly but could digest my food with care. The course was finished and I returned to find a lot of things wrong, and was very worried.

RAF Hixon

I was posted to RAF Hixon, North Stafford, which shook me — pottery country. Vera was posted to Swinderby, North Lincoln, which was a good station. When my train arrived at Stafford, I got my cases and kit bag on to a trolley, past the ticket collector. There was transport and more RAF drifted through. Across the way was a large hotel, which I found out later was a good place to get a hot cup of something and the bar was usually open, a better room than the stark railway station.

It was bitterly cold. There were many WAAF Officers in different branches. RAF and WAAF officers all messed together and queued up for meals. The camp was eight miles from the town, and the satellite station was quite a few miles away on a lonely site.

There was one big plus: the RAF Officers, especially the C.O. and the Chaplain, were terrific blokes. At my initiation I was told I would not be there long and they knew I had three weeks' leave due. It was nice to see the rolling hills and countryside but the cold was intense — I learned that Stoke-on-Trent and Birmingham were not far away.

I knew I was not there for promotion, but I could see there was an awful lot of work to be done. I soon saw discipline was slack, there were many absentees due to the conscript system. There was a listless feeling among the whole WAAF unit. I thought to myself, I am only here for a few weeks; this station should have every advantage. The C.O. was a pilot, charming, and the Chaplain was in good form. It was part of Bomber Command — an OCTU (Officers Training Unit) with special duties. The planes flew over border-line areas around the enemy, dropping leaflets to the civilians and to the Germans to give themselves up, also bagfuls of nickel; the strips of metal were skillfully eased out in streams to cut their radar signals; of course, Command regulated the times.

We had a very short Sunday Parade and Service and the WAAF officers and others were asked to have a drink with the C.O. I have to admit the WAAF NCOs were either quite incompetent or very depressed. The way things were, they were not overworked.

When I had been round the main camp, I thought I would try and see what was lacking at the satellite, a set of huts up on a flat top hill. The sergeant showed me round. I checked all the factual things like lights functioning and ablutions — everything was depressingly ordinary. The Sergeant made no comments about anything at all.

My routine was to walk up to the mess at 8a.m., have breakfast and go up to the offices, lunch at 12.30 and work until 5.30, have tea, walk down to the WAAF mess and return for dinner at 7.30p.m. I met an officer who was an airman with me at Detling; a Warrant Officer who was a Sergeant over me, also at Detling; and an officer who was an airwoman at Detling and was later killed flying on duty, only 21, and a very nice person. Her father kept a stationer's shop in Maidstone, she had just married an Army officer who had gone out to India. She was buried with full military honours.

I could not wear my battle dress as it was not considered an operational place. The food was very good. Sleep was impossible until midnight; we were in a Nissan hut with a corridor along the length, so anyone coming in slammed the entrance door.

There was a railway line along a boundary with some WAAF quarters and a small chapel and Padre's quarters, plus other buildings. On the other side of the line there were quarters for the OCTU training officers. The batwomen left the quarters with their NCO about 12 noon, the time when an express train came through; apart from the whistling shriek, you could hear it coming — the gates were permanently shut, but there were the two pedestrian gates to be opened and shut.

I thought I would look in at the chapel and as I came out I heard the train coming. I strolled over and to my horror saw the small gate open on the other side, and a WAAF walked into the train. I steeled myself to cross the lines. I put my arm up to the other WAAFs to stay where they were. It was needless, they were stupefied. On their side about 15 feet away the WAAF lay on her back, peacefully. I made sure she was dead and put my jacket over her. I walked along to the airwomen and asked the NCO to take her girls over and ring the

M.O., then the C.O. on my behalf, I would stay with the poor child. A small crowd gathered the other side. It was not many minutes, but it seemed hours, until I was relieved.

Out of all this several of the batwomen asked to see me: "You see ma'am, we all knew she was deaf, never knew how she passed her medical, she just always smiled and said, "Yes." I was more than shocked. The Chaplain and I had to tell the parents, a stolid, elderly couple. A sergeant came to me and handed over quite an amazing packet of money, saying, "We passed the hat round for the parents." The C.O. had more than he had bargained for — neither of us could understand how on earth that airwoman could sail through the service's strict medicals. So we had another funeral when permitted by the coroner and police.

One Christmas I had leave to go home, and working out a difficult timetable, I could just arrive at Penzance in the evening in time for the last bus. I had my kit-bag, a medium-sized case and the usual gas mask.

I was travelling from the north via Wolverhampton, on to Plymouth, and to Penzance. It was bitterly cold weather, the train seemed only half heated and was absolutely full of soldiers with full kit. I cannot remember for certain which camp I was on or which railway station I got on; it was possibly Hixon. I got a seat, travelling first class, only just. The corridors were packed. We slowed down at Wolverhampton. We were ordered out of the train and the chap behind the megaphone told us to take cover, and that is where we would be staying the night. The Germans were flying overhead, a few bombs were dropped, the train moved off to a side-line. We had water but there was no food. Throughout everyone was good-natured, though everyone seemed to be exhausted. Kit-bags were used as pillows, and we were packed like sardines which kept us warm. About 4a.m. the megaphone aroused us. A train came in; I saw some officers and edged up to them as we crammed into carriages. By this time some personnel had departed.

Eventually, as we approached Plymouth, we started and stopped. Great flames in patches were alight. They had been severely bombed. Then after a time we stopped in the station and the Mayor of Plymouth and a team of Salvation Army and WVS were there to greet us with hot drinks, sandwich packets and some kind of mince pies. Those who were going to Penzance or near were asked to go into a van or car and were taken to the famous Hoe, where there were seats and a view of the sea, apparently where Sir Walter Raleigh was reputed to be playing bowls when the Armada was sighted. There was one WAAF, one airman and two soldiers, different regiments. We were to amuse ourselves but not go out of sight because a bus would (or might) pick us up at 2p.m. The sun was out, the WAAF saw some public toilets so we agreed to go in separately and be responsible for each other, as the bus could come in earlier. Each of us had strange tales to tell; the men were particularly keen on their families. We all agreed it was a very pleasant break until the bus came. We were told that the railway bridge that goes to Devonport over the river, then to Cornwall, was bombed. A row of buses was at the station. We would go up a road to the nearest bridge inland and by bus down to the other side of Devonport. What a Christmas Day! I arrived in Penzance at 9.30a.m. on Boxing Day. There were a few tradesmen's vans but nearly all our passengers had got off by the time we came to the end. I piled my stuff by the ticket office and found a truck whose driver would extend his run and take me over to Gurnards Head.

There were quite a few people killed in that raid and the Germans had tried to bomb the station but missed. There was hardly a grumble but plenty of ribbing and joking amongst the soldiers, who knew each other. My mother was glad to see me. I could not phone, the lines were badly damaged in Plymouth and we saw one oil tank ablaze near the end of the cliffs.

RAF Oakington

I reported back to Group HQ and found I was going to RAF Oakington, a bomber station near Cambridge. It was a very efficient, busy place. WAAF officers were in a house at the end of the village, with a nice garden and rooms. We biked into the RAF mess and back, and to our work. I had a lot to do with a number of WAAF in many trades: three cipher officers, one catering, and good administrative officers. There were two regular squadrons of Lancasters, plus a Mosquito Pathfinder squadron, and later visiting American Fortresses, huge ugly planes. They belonged to the USA. Our airmen came from New Zealand, Australia, and Canada, apart from our own men.

I think an outsider at this stage should realise the enormous importance of our duties. The Code and Cipher Officers were very competent in their work, skilled in mathematics and very silent, rightly so. Also they escaped the emotional side of WAAF life and were not in charge of individuals who were in distress, but they had to keep to themselves the code of secrecy of what the enemy might or might not do. Also except for a few of them, they hardly got much promotion. For one thing, most of them did not care because they had a private income, and another they were in a professional, intellectual job.

When I arrived I saw, as a newcomer, many things that could help the airwomen; improving their quarters and surrounds, extra security and pleasant off-duty places to relax in their quarters.

The WAAF quarters, like the officers', were in the village at opposite ends, but the officers were in an established house. The airwomen were in recently built huts, just placed on a down-graded site off the road that led into the village. In the entrance, on the right, were amenity huts with no amenities yet, so no one used them. I personally had to settle in and get to know my opposite numbers to get things done.

Night bombing raids were being devastating to the enemy, so a relative proportion of women were on night duty. When they came off duty in the early morning on rainy days, they did not want to get to their huts in mud. So unofficially, I got the NCOs together off-duty to discuss how we could get the entrance and all the surrounding areas of the huts levelled-up and free of mud. I waited, I put in the ideas: how long had the solid piles of gravel, now greening, lain unused on the eastern side, near the ammunition dump? How much gravel was used every month or quarter from the mounting stockpile? I got to know the Department of Works men in charge, so a plan unfolded.

All volunteer airwomen were asked to clear weeds from around their huts after tea within a week. I had a stock plumbing inspection for leaking pipes and tap washers, and got everything that ought to be done fixed

233

at once, so nothing had to be dug up. We needed three non-operational nights, three truck drivers and large rollers attached to the tractor to make a good, hard, compacted, gravel surrounding. All without being officially noticed. It was a very, very anxious time. New boyfriends turned up and silently filled corners in with spades. Our entrance was shaped, a new drain and drainpipes put in.

I personally fetched paint from stores and borrowed brushes, and over a weekend we painted our amenity huts. The airwomen were thrilled — no muddy shoes. In the future, we got weekly information bulletins on the amenity board; I collected clean magazines, and a few writing tables (legitimately) from Stores, and easy chairs. The last touches were a few flower boxes, and then the place look civilised.

I dreaded the CO's monthly inspection. He pretended there was no difference, but inspected the sanitation and electric lights: one lavatory bulb had gone and one tap needed a washer. Men are very perverse, I took note and said to my Sergeant, "See that is fixed." The C.O. said, "I see you have cleaned the place up, about time." I escorted him back to his office. He gave me a funny look.

I worked into the variable routines. I was usually Duty Officer every four or five days.

The whole of Britain was inundated with the awareness of enemy parachutists. Naturally the Press printed very amusing cartoons, and the government issued small posters. So I had my fright on a duty round. Right beyond the WAAF site was an orchard established along the railway line, with the boundary of the camp on its other side. The orchard gate was on my right side. My patrol stopped over the railway line, past two fields to a large house which the RAF had seconded to house groups of WAAF shift-workers. Each night a woman Duty Officer glanced in and walked discreetly around, noting the time.

So this balmy night, about 11p.m., it was bright moonlight, I looked in utter amazement — there were rows and rows of white tents through the orchard. A tall soldier was on guard by the gate with a small makeshift hut. The man was a very, very dark Negro. In our warning the Germans were disguising their spy parachutists by blackening their faces.

So I carefully laid my bike down on the bank and drew my large torch out; I had my tin hat on. I went up to the soldier who had an American uniform on and said, "Good evening soldier, what is all this? What unit? Can I speak to your officer in charge, please? I am Duty Officer and you are on prohibited property." He looked dazed, so I said, "Aren't you taught to stand to attention when you are spoken to by an officer?" He straightened up and moved to his hut and spoke in his field telephone, he said someone was coming; he looked at me, then at his watch and the railway line. An American officer strolled up, and I said, "Can you tell me what is going on?" He smiled and said, "No, I can't." So I said, "Can you show me who you are?" and he did produce his I.D. card, saying, "Look, it's OK." So I just nodded and I said to myself, "There are only rifles, there are not any frightening weapons," so as

235

soon as I reached the "WAAFery" I phoned to the RAF Duty Officer on the main camp, who was quite shocked. He said, "I'll ring the old man (the C.O.)." I went round the quarters, woke an NCO and said, "There is an American unit in the orchard, they are harmless but I shall be meeting the C.O. at the railway line in a few minutes."

Apparently the Americans were running a train load of ammunitions through that evening, and they had posses of troops at intervals to make sure everything was guarded. They never even gave the RAF a thought! Of course high up there were repercussions. But I got a fright at first.

I wrote about the shocking traffic problems in England, to my mother:

Cornwall must be full of visitors now, packed and overflowing. Heaven knows what would happen if the Armistice came before the cold weather. Traffic by air would be impossible. I am sticking like glue to my service bike, it gets trundled in and out of planes, strung by wire, to bits and pieces of fuselage.

I am organising all sorts of classes this autumn for the WAAF — even if peace comes in Europe we shall still have to knit, sew and carpenter for the continentals. I have got a lovely workshop built in one of the disused ablutions. Now the war is finished I shall not get my extra ring, but it is better to be a FI/O in the country than a Sq/Officer in a large city.

I mentioned that Cambridge railway station was as unbelievable as the London stations — the congestion was caused by parents going madly in and from the country to visit their billeted children and relations.

The Normans are doubtful whether they are pleased with the Allies using their countryside as a battleground. I've seen some illuminating talks with the boys returned already on sick leave. The Parisians will without doubt be delighted and wild with joy when we enter Paris. It can only be weeks now for that, and a German collapse, we may hope for another 11 November.

The C.O. sent for me and told me under terrific secrecy that the King, the Queen and the two Princesses were paying us a visit in two or three days and that there would be an investiture held between the hangars. I had to get the large ante-room ready for tea; a group of young pilot officers would be presented to the princesses, separated from the King; the A.O.C. and the C.O. would sit apart, and various officers would be summoned; the Queen and I would sit at a small table apart in another area, and I would present the WAAF officers gradually. I was to organise the tea and accoutrements (there were none!)

S.O. White (catering officer) organised the tea; I had called on likely people in the village to lend some small tablecloths, decent cigarette boxes and small flower vases. I made a list and said I made myself responsible for their safe return.

The Royals went round the hangars and saw the squadrons in full flying rig and ground crew and the Ops room. I was to wait on the steps at the mess to receive the party to be presented and usher the Queen and her Lady-in-Waiting to the cloakroom, a meagre little place with two basins and two lavatories; I managed to borrow some decent hand-towels. The Queen said, "Oh, Flight Officer, how extravagant — *two* tablets of soap, we can share." She was smiling; I bowed and said, "I shall be outside the door if you want anything."

The Lady-in-Waiting opened the door and I ushered them into the ante-room, and introduced her to S.O. White who had organised the kitchen to make thin sandwiches, scones and, to my amazement, some dainty small cakes. Also we had managed to borrow a few decent teapots.

Conversation with Her Majesty was so easy, she discussed the flowers and the different trades of the WAAF, in between people coming up to meet her. She asked for the recipe for the cakes — she wanted to know if she could have one. I got the senior Cipher Officer to take my place and went into the kitchen and asked the Sergeant who had produced the recipe; a very shy girl came forward and I told her to write it down and put her name at the end. I said, "You will all be presented in the main hall upon Their Majesties' departure", and to the WAAF, "Be prepared to give your recipe yourself."

The two Princesses were not shy with the surrounding young men and were laughing; I thought Princess Elizabeth looked small and slight.

The A.O.C., the King and the C.O. began to depart, and the Queen and her Lady-in-Waiting, who was absolutely delightful, drifted into the main entrance. It was wonderful to see the wide-eyed cooks and kitchen hands grouped together. The Queen spoke to them all, and the shy WAAF was there. I beckoned her out, she curtsied and handed her recipe to Her Majesty, who asked after her family; and we had to get on with the departure cars and so they drove away.

I rushed back to make a special place to check all our borrowed articles and locked them up for their safe return. The A.O.C. had gone back to group. By then the whole village had turned out and lined the road, so I was told. The Group Captain looked very tired, he took me down to his caravan where his wife was staying and he then cooked us all a lovely egg-and-bacon supper.

One of my pleasurable duties was that on my Sunday off I would go to Ely Military Hospital and visit our patients, usually they were overseas flying personnel. Someone used to put a note up in the mess board when the car was leaving. I went every Sunday depending who was there. One young New Zealand crewman had so many multiple fractures that no one thought he could live, he was in traction at such an angle that it was hard to hear him. He liked me to read the letters he had received. I used to make up letters to send as he slowly spoke.

If there was time, I used to visit Ely Cathedral nearby. On one or two Sundays I went to King's College and sometimes I was lucky to hear them sing in the early evening. I used to catch the bus for those sorts of outings. Of course all the shops were shut.

In the summer when Ops were not on, some of us used to go to the out-of-the-way pubs. When Ops. was on, usually three of us non-Cipher Officers (meaning Administration) were rostered, one each night or early morning to ration out a strict measure of rum with a mug of hot coffee whilst the crew was de-briefed. The trick was, there were five men and they stood in turn and then joined the end to get another tot of rum.

The WAAF officer on duty used to rest early, depending where they were bombing and returning from midnight to pre-daylight hours.

One morning about 1a.m. I cut through a small wood, a well trampled short cut, one lifted one's bike over the bent wire. A dark figure loomed up and said, "Who's there?" It was our local policeman on his round. Just as we were getting acquainted, I heard our first plane coming in and I said to the bobby, "Help me over or I will be late." Then I heard the whine and alien engines. The policeman was over like a flash to drag me back. We were too late, a Dornier came in above the landing of our planes. I lay down and buried my head, a bomb exploded nearly tearing our guts out. I opened my eyes and saw a white, gleaming river pouring towards us. I said to my friend, "Quick, get up, they've hit the paint store.".We circled round the crater and the policeman said, "My wife will kill me if I don't take a souvenir." He was scrabbling down the side. I told him to get me a piece too, with gloves; it would be scorching. I wrapped my piece up and biked quickly to the tarmac, and stopped a vehicle. One WAAF was hurt and on her way to sick quarters. I got into the ops area much dishevelled and with paint splashed on my battledress top. I had to move quickly, scrubbed up, the urn was bubbling and the first crew came in as I unfastened the rum cupboard. I said to them, "You need not have asked the Jerries in too." The crew said, "There was only one plane and our defence will get him going back."

There was one advantage. When all the crews were in — we waited in case the overdues could make it — we all trailed to the mess, where the heroes who came back tucked in to full flying breakfast, with the rum-givers included: bacon, eggs, tomatoes and chips etc.

All this time I was getting regular letters from James Floyd who was released before me. After all he had served well in France in World War I and had been slightly gassed. Margaret Sims sent vague messages from Wales, but it was a while before we met again. I did get in some flying with my very busy C.O., but not much. I hardly saw the Pathfinder Mosquitoes; they were very special planes and closely guarded.

I received the following letter from my friend, Section Officer Jean V. G. Crawford who was serving in Canada at this time:

I was so glad to hear from you. I get very lonely for Oakington, so you can well imagine in spite of

241

the fact that I would wish to be there I could never go back. Sometimes fate works in a strange way.

I try to work up some enthusiasm for my work here, but one is only part of a machine and the human element is non-existent. However, perhaps it all a means to an end and easier in the long run. I am to move away from Montreal pretty soon — one's tour should consist of nine months and I've already done six. I shall then go on to some out-station which will be a great opportunity to see some of these out-of-the-way places one reads about but never dreams of seeing. By rights I should be in Brazil by now but A.M. are still tossing up as to what it is suitable for females, men having been there previously. Three of us were to go and it would have been quite an experience — especially the 5000-mile journey by plane. I am still hoping it will come off but at this stage of the war I doubt it.

What reaction do you get when you think of living in a world not at war? Mine is in a way a very strange lost one as so many lives have been altered, and there will be so much to face up to won't there? Surely the Germans can't last much longer. Don't lose heart Daphne dear please, I want you to be happy.

Then follows a list of queries about our officers; she mentions lack of promotion but good overseas allowance pay.

Crawford sent a second letter shortly after:

There is a great amount of work to do. Shopping is very strange and it is difficult not to ask with the usual apology in one's voice. "How many can I have?" or "May I have two?" — everything is very plentiful and the shops full, and full of the luxuries long forgotten . . . The shortage of cipher officers over here is fantastic, when you think of the large number in the UK doing nothing at all.. I can't tell you how much I miss an operational station. I hate being out of the war. At least you stand more chance of killing all those Germans you said you would . . . I met a PFF (Pathfinder) type at a party the other night and my word was I glad to see him.

It is strange to eat ice cream, oranges, bananas, white bread and eggs. I hope you have got a good S.O, at least she can't be as frightful as B — . Don't worry over everything that crops up and DON'T look for work as you do. Jean

This shows the differences of living on the edge in the United Kingdom and the luxury of Canada and USA. The happy ending is that Jean is happily married to her ex-airman; they tend their magnificent rose garden in Hampshire, with children abroad.

The war was near the end and I was soon posted to Henlow Training Depot, where they were reversing the situation, with vocational training for the massive restoring of the services to work.

RAF Henlow

I had some leave in Cornwall and left to go to London, then on to RAF Henlow on the outskirts of Hitchin, Hertfordshire. Henlow was a very large training centre for all ranks in different trades, including overseas countries — about 8,000 personnel, including 800 WAAF. There was a railway line, an offshoot from the mainline into the side of the camp.

Everywhere was spick and span. The Administration building was large. I reported to the Station Commanding Officer, Air Commodore Townsend, who had his wings up; very courteous. I would be working for Squadron Officer Benson and be in charge when she was away. The WAAF officers had their own house, and a woman doctor was quartered with us. We had breakfast there but the rest of our meals would be in the large RAF mess. There were two hospitals and RAF sick quarters. The Queen Mary Nurses' Home was near us but they were self-sufficient with their matron.

There was a separate contingent of several hundred Jamaicans who were Sergeants or Flight Sergeants who had completed their flying training. Their commissions were suspended, as the war was bound to be over that year, so these men were just put there. They were under their own C.O., Wing Commander Wyndham Goldie, an actor. No airwomen were allowed in their camp, except WAAF officers on duty.

Then Air Commodore Townsend introduced me to Squadron Officer Benson; she was middle aged and could have been one of my aunts. She had the Benson features, more like Aunt Olive. She looked severe, but I felt more at ease with her than she was with me. I was to have the office next door and would be doing a lot of accommodation inspections, running the airwomen's activities and dealing with the girls' welfare on a day-to-day basis. As it was such a large place, at first I was to be taken to visit the heads of sections, mostly by the RAF. I gathered the Squadron Officer would be away quite a bit.

I told her I had a licence for different vehicles, but she said there was an abundance of M.T. drivers and there would be no need for me to drive. I knew I would work well with the C.O., the Admin. Wing Officer, and the Adjutant, they were all very likeable men. I put my gear away in a modern house like the larger married quarters in Uxbridge. By that time it was lunch-hour when I was introduced to the messing routine. It was wonderful not to feel raids were imminent and that one had to be alert for attacks, but there would be an awful lot of people to disperse at the end of the year.

Fortunately, I was fit and ready to contribute to the new Air Ministry orders on Vocational Training. So far no plans had been put into place. We were fortunate in being so near to London and having access to trained people.

Towards the end of March, I was excused all duties for 36 hours: the laryngitis complaint cropped up again. I could not even get a growl out, so parades and telephones were out of range.

As soon as I felt better I wrote a letter to my mother (1 April):

I have been kept very busy, the Squadron Officer is away for 14 days. I have four officers ill as we've had a small epidemic in the Mess. I am coming down in April but we think the "cease fire" might be through next weekend, as there is no German High Command and no government. Our Jamaican contingent are getting restless and impatient for release, which is natural. Many of them were highly skilled and educated men.

We were all asked if we would be willing to join the occupation force. I volunteered to stay on, but not overseas. I managed to visit W.C. Wyndham Goldie every week, choosing books for him that he might not have read, we had quite an amicable time discussing books. At Easter, I visited all the patients in the two hospitals and the sick quarters, which was in quarantine.

One hospital was allocated to German officer patients who had long-term treatment. I visited an injured doctor, he was conscripted into the Army; he was a rheumatologist with a private practice and family. I used to supply him with books. He told me of a simple way to relieve my arthritis; it worked. He was elderly, a loyal German but not of Hitler's kind.

Cease Fire

After the Cease Fire, we had a Drumhead Service in the morning. Later we went to the mess dance and visited all the other messes, and eventually all ranks danced on the cricket pitch.

2 September 1945:

Waiting for the announcement has been harrowing for all personnel — the men and the extrovert women have cast off their cares; it's like a tenseness before a race.

From what I remember the announcement was made that trains would be available from our Station direct to London. Personnel were advised not to get too carried away but to return to camp for duty and continue to be demobilised.

00.30 hours. The war is over. I had been fast asleep and suddenly phones were ringing, then silence. The sisters from the Hospital Mess dragged me out of bed and I went over and had a beer with them in my pyjamas. The WAAF officers went to sleep and were not demonstrative.

247

Anyway that is the end of war. The mopping up will now begin. I hope our prisoners will not lose their lives. I think the Japanese will betray us wholesale.

We are not allowed outside a zone of 20 miles — even to the last we have to be regulated. Needless to say the troops will all pour into London regardless.

On VJ Day, 1945 at RAF Station, Henlow, we held a service of Thanksgiving and Dedication. The hymn was "New Every Morning", five short prayers, the Lord's Prayer, St Luke Chapter 2: 8-14. Padre gave an address. Then we sang the hymn, "O God our Help in Ages Past", then there was the Blessing and the National Anthem.

On the Thursday after I went up to London; my interview and board were cancelled but as I had an appointment with Alec (Beecham) to lunch in the House and attend a debate, I went up. The Prime Minister was speaking in the afternoon, but he was so tired that I could hardly hear him. Later, after I got my books for my course on Vocational Training, I met Alec, Betty Poulson from Buryan, and Mr. Nicklin, a solicitor from St Just; we all had dinner at the Ambassador Club, which was fine. I returned straight to camp, as I had to work on Saturday and Sunday; the Squadron Officer was going away on her Easter grant of three days plus the Victory 48 hours.

Squadron Officer Holmes (Air Ministry) had been posted to India and was flying off on the 27th. I had to attend an E.V.T. (Educational Training Course) School on 17th, flying to Ringway on 16th, then train or transport to Manchester, flying back on 18th.

I went to Bedford and bought a dress length with service coupons and stockings, and this little triumph cheered me up amidst all this uncertainty for the future. Everyone was allowed to wear civilian clothes after duty and go off on leave or pass.

Many peacetime regulations were returning and it was very strange after severe, rigid rules. On the Monday I had to take off by car, starting at 06.45, to a conference at Farnborough at Command HQ, as the Squadron Officer was not well enough, returning at 11p.m. I saw Barnes and Group Officer McAlery, which was good, all of us ex-West Drayton.

The Air Commodore asked me whether I would accept an invitation to tea in Hitchin with the Bowes-Lyon sisters; they were quite near and would like to entertain one of us. The C.O. said he would get the Adjutant to fix up a car and driver to get there by 4p.m. and pick me up by 5.30p.m., or I could go earlier if I wished to shop in Hitchin. I said I would like to wander along the main street. So I did that. David Bowes-Lyon is the President of the Royal Horticultural Society and he is the eldest of the family, cousins of the Queen. It is a very old house of great charm, with a lovely front garden with two herbaceous borders. We had a lovely but simple tea; one of the sisters had made the scones. We were in the garden, talking plants, and I found a lot of old-fashioned treasures. As I was leaving I was

249

presented with a large goose egg, enough for a large pancake for five, a very precious gift. I shall never forget the peace and quiet of that lovely old home — civilisation.

PART THREE

The Post-War Years

Planning for De-mobilisation

Dear mother, I have been desperately busy lately. The new Squadron Officer is installed. We gather that out of 14 WAAF officers, there will be three of us to cope, unless there are any replacements. I have been organising a big fashion parade via John Lewis of Oxford Street. They are sending a manager (and staff) to check details. The subject is "Your wardrobe upon Release" and they are sending a team of mannequins to show garments. We are having three performances.

I shall never forget Henlow, never. I think of our Mannequin Parade, which was a great success. The Manager, Mrs. Paget, and her assistant Mrs. Bye, Assistant Manager of Sales, planned all the garments, sizes and prices on the racks we had fixed up in our recreation/meeting hut. She called for and asked several WAAF to join in a show of clothes. In her introduction she outlined the staff positions and the conditions of work, if they applied for jobs. The John Lewis group gave the women an uplifting feeling with regards to getting work.

By now, I had abolished the traditional Domestic Evenings. One evening a week, all airwomen had to go through their kit and do their mending; if they had done this they could attend a class of sewing, toy making, it depended on whom I could find to teach. Of course the uncertainty of the future made us very edgy. I tried to be calm and reassuring, but I had problems at home and no future, as I kept on being inoculated or vaccinated for every tropical or current disease. I had the problem of getting our tenants out of our own place in Cornwall; they were bombarded with solicitors' letters with suggestions, even where they could store their own things in Truro. Meanwhile the Shipping Department wanted my mother out, ready for the proposed return of the Coastguards.

I went up to town to spend the day with Section Officer Millar and her mother. Her father, Dr. Morrieston Davies was a consulting tuberculosis surgeon for the RAF and had been looking after my cousin Georgina (WAAF). Brenda Millar was at school with all the Ticehursts in Cheltenham. The following weekend was quite a momentous one for me. It was Feast Day at Coombe, Oxford. I had been in touch with Gladys who worked for us at the Vicarage. She married Lionel, who was in the choir; they had a son and lived at the Mill near the Halt on the railway line. I took Vera down, a constantly ill friend who was at Snaith with me. Gladys gave us a great welcome and quite a few people came to welcome me.

I wanted to see whether Vera and Gladys got on as it would be somewhere for Vera to recuperate. I honestly cannot remember whether she did or not. But our weekend was a great success. I returned to Henlow to find that our Matron had been posted to Yatesbury. Up to now she was ill in our hospital and could not take an interest in anything. We tried everything. I took her my seaweed collection, which she busily sorted out in bed and attached their labels. At least it was something and she seemed to enjoy the beautiful patterned plants — at last it was a breakthrough.

I understand Alec is getting me a seat in the House for the Opening in the Royal Gallery. We are in a muddle! All our domestic trades are getting married. Masses of technical airwomen are being posted in, and the key men are being posted or released. I should have been released with our remaining two, but we have been told it is our duty to remain! Labour is in, but Alec has kept his seat with a good majority, but of course he won't be appointed Lord of the Treasury now. With Labour, they have promised equal pay for equal work . . . The Squadron Officer is being admitted to hospital for three weeks and I suppose she will have sick leave.

10,000 civilians swarmed around the camp for Open Day! It was all over by 6p.m. The following day I went to Henlow Parish Church for a combined Harvest Thanksgiving and Air Force Service.

I have to take two visiting Group Officers around the camp. We have a new Station Administrative Officer, Wing Commander Shore, an ex-POW, incredibly young. Being a pilot he said he would fly me to Manchester to my meeting. He has a lovely car which I am allowed to drive; I have visited his wife who is in a London hospital.

I wrote home to warn my mother to visit the coal-man and give her order for the future, and also to get some more paraffin cans filled. Heating would be a future problem.

I was starting a cooking school through the Ministry of Labour and the Ministry of Food, who were sending instructors three days a week. The other trades needed for the future were bricklayers, painters and plumbers, so I passed that on to the RAF Education Officer.

The Air Ministry had not given any indication on what it wanted to do about those left. I had my medical and appeared to be as good as out. Group HQ had no idea if we were being kept on, so I enquired about particulars for an airline hostess in British-Latin Airways Ltd., Housing Management for the L.C.C., UNRA Army of Occupation, Rehabilitation Personnel Management, Transport, and so on. I thought John Lewis might give me a job in an emergency.

The interview with John Lewis was interesting but not lucrative. First, it was in the printing and photography control office, the work was detailed, ending up in write-ups in *Tailor and Cutter*, *Vogue*, and so on. Until I mastered the printing side, the consideration was £6/-/- a week, with a final prospect of £500/-/-. At that time, release seemed to be in December but was not yet confirmed.

The Gaiety Show

Arthur Howard, the brother of Leslie Howard, an actor in his own right, started The Gaiety Old-Time Music Hall. He is a fantastic stage director, and also presented Dave Aylott's *Riding Higher* earlier on. They had a wonderful cast and on 6th December 1945 presented the *Gaiety Show*, with the authors Derek Waterlow and Frank Muir.

F.Lt. Howard was a friend of mine who had asked me to help with his concerts — he asked me to be his hostess on his last night of the Gaiety. Service people, unless they are brought up in the entertaining world, do not understand the hard work at all times, and the involvement in the right places. For this day I met the 7p.m. train, met Jean Compton MacKenzie, Arthur's wife and the actress, and took her to the theatre. I then looked after Claude Hulbert, his wife Enid Trevor, and their daughter Colman. Enid was very beautiful and charming, and was very unassuming. After the show I took them over to the RAF Mess dance, it was nearly midnight. My few remaining friends were still there, Group Captain Stokes and his wife and Leslie Styles and his wife. What amused me was the room was packed and several remarks were made about their heavy make-up. Suddenly after half an hour, people realised they had come straight off the stage and they all rushed for introductions.

Arthur was rather done in as he had been working very hard on three shows with the entertainment officer. He was exactly like his brother Leslie Howard, who was tragically killed in a plane accident later on. Enid Trevor asked me what I was doing after release and laughingly said, "Come with us to Germany and be our family Secretary." The Hulberts returned home by car. I put Jean, Arthur's wife, to bed, as we had spare rooms. She had a streaming cold and felt rotten. She stayed a few days until she unwound. She told me quite a bit about her father, the writer.

My programme was covered with signatures: Claude Hulbert and his wife; Jean Compton MacKenzie, the daughter of the author; Christina M. MacQueen; Daphne Tanner, the dancer; Irene Howard; Dorothea Wilson; and a lot of stage people from the service.

The Squadron Officer returned on the Thursday; I was very rushed trying to pack. On Friday we had a few drinks in the mess. I was trying to pack again, but there were masses of forms to sign. At 6p.m. I invited the C.O. and a few officers and my theatre crowd who are on the camp for a few days, to the Ladies Room for supper at 8p.m. in the WAAF Sergeants Mess with my guests. I fetched Arthur Howard, Derek Waterlow and Daphne Tanner, who had got me an interview with Fortnum and Mason.

Job Hunting

I met Leslie Styles' brother, a manager of Kodak, and had lunch at the Savoy. I had left nearly all my things at the Club on my way to be demobbed in Birmingham on the Tuesday. That night I was staying with some actors from Henlow.

I returned to the Club and seriously got down to job hunting whilst I was in London — an exhausting and painful experience. I had entertained a journalist from the *Sunday Empire News*, as the Squadron Officer was on sick leave again. Afterwards I surprisingly got an invitation to dinner in town. I was offered £5/-/- a week for being a secretary and office worker in the Queen's Nursing Institute and Midwives Hostel in Chelsea. If our home were in Chelsea I would have taken it. If things got sticky over our accommodation, I thought they might release me in November.

I then outlined to my mother what I had done with the solicitors over the occupation of the St Agnes cottage, and told the tenants that they would be up for the payment of storage for our furniture:

If we get moving an ex-WAAF has written to me for a domestic job, she lives at Scorrier, so I would have to find her digs in the village. Also I have a cook who wants to work in Bath. She would suit your two Bath friends. The Housing Estate Centre has interviewed me, it would be very hard work, but worthwhile; the training is 18 months, but no pay ... I am trying to fly down in a Mosquito to Portreath Wednesday/Thursday and quickly visit our tenants. Of course it depends on the weather. It's only 40 minutes away at 350 mph. So if you see a two-engined aircraft with a stiff short tail round the coast guard, you know it's me with my POW friend — weather permitting. Don't worry, I'll get the tenants out if we have to dive-bomb them out.

On 26 January I wrote to Cornwall to say that I had been staying with the Ellard-Styles; he was a regular RAF engineer at Henlow.

I had my board eventually with the Prison Commissioners at the Home Office and was being considered as a House Mistress, later converted to the title of Assistant Governor. It would be long hours and a tough job behind prison walls. I liked the Commissioners especially the woman Commissioner, all utterly dedicated to the care and training of Borstal girls and Star Prisoners for the future. So the next step would be call-up for a medical board to the place nearest to my home.

The search for work tailed off, apart from my willingness to tackle anything with an interesting future, including training. It boiled down to two things:

we had got possession of "Trevaunance", the St Agnes cottage and were in the midst of revamping it, and found that London suburbia was cheaper for ironmongery, from nuts and bolts to house steps, etc.

I had trudged through every kind of interview; it came to needing a permanent roof over my head and enough to assist materially with our home in Cornwall. I was not depressed or scared at all the refusals or impossible conditions, because to quote from a letter I wrote to my mother on 26 January 1946:

I knew everything would be very hard. I've met several qualified ex-WREN officers with degrees and full shorthand; they have been out of work for weeks and weeks.

In trades, businesses and professions it was all difficult; one young man who saw me said, "As far as we are concerned you have been 'out' for nearly seven years, so you are all a dead loss and have to start at the bottom." That did not hit me, but I felt very sad for all the servicemen and -women who had come back to nothing — injured, lost homes, and no work. My tally of applications with hopes and replies was forty-three!

Prison Service

I had an interview with a Prison Commissioner at the Home Office; she was very charming and a genuinely nice person. She said that she would like me to work for her and that she would try and convene a Board Meeting before I returned to Cornwall, to save travelling.

Whilst waiting, I made an appointment at P5 (Personnel) Air Ministry to find that my ex-WAAF C.O., whose husband was a Director of a brewery, still wanted someone to run their canteen; there would also be promotion from there to other things. Starting pay would be at £7/-/- per week and I fixed an interview for Friday. Yes, I could be interested in brewing! At Ditton Court Farm we grew hops to perfection for the Maidstone Brewery; I had learnt about the American Golden Hops, the varieties, soils, and how they all contribute to locality brewing. This did not solve my Cornish dilemma. The location of the brewery was in Fulham, and providing lodgings for myself would not leave any surplus for the home in St Agnes. In the meantime I accidentally met Mrs. Paget, the Personnel and Training Manager of John Lewis, who had staged the Henlow mannequin show. I was shocked at her appearance and her despair and sadness through disillusionment. She had returned to her flat in London and now she was just doing store work in John Lewis. Anyway we settled down and I gave her a few introductions including to the BBC, especially to Mrs. Wyndham Goldie, the wife of the C.O. who controlled the Jamaican unit at Henlow. Mrs. Goldie was the BBC's Women's Editor of a daily series and had her own section. As we were doing this, the BBC rang up and could give me a night printer's job, which I declined. I had had enough of night work on our Bomber Stations and had slept badly ever since.

The Station Commanding Officer, Air Commodore, had written a very good testimonial for the Prison Service. The advantage was that the staff had rooms available for friends and relatives to stay in the staff quarters overnight or for a few days. Employees had one month's leave, all medical expenses covered, sick leave, and a furnished bed-sitting room or three unfurnished rooms with full facilities.

I was to go to Aylesbury for training, then Kent, with the promise of promotion; apparently they could not get people to go into the service, losing staff through marriage. It was not a career I would have chosen but I was used to guards, police and barbed wire and miles of regulations. The quarters were outside the prison walls, but I could see the greater part of the prison from my windows.

I had my Board interview, subject to passing my medical, which would be in the south-west. I went down to Cornwall — to Redruth by train, and changed there for the bus to St Agnes. My mother was very anxious of course, and quite stunned by my working in a prison.

It was not long before I was sent a return railway warrant to Princetown, where I would be met. I was to report to the Governor of H.M. Prison, Dartmoor, the most written-about and historical of all prisons. I was very intrigued to say the least. As I was acknowledging the letter, I had a note from the Governor saying that after my Board, he and his wife hoped I would stay for lunch — all very civilised.

A car driven by a prison officer (in mufti) met me at Princetown. There was a sense of isolation in the beautiful but forbidding moors, according to the mood of the weather. There were huge, grey, thick walls with double gates, as with all prisons. I was taken straight through to the Prison Hospital, where there were two doctors, both male. I went through the familiar routine with my demobilisation medical report, but there was a clause which I had not realised: I was still in a Z force, which meant I could be called up for civilian or service duties in the case of an emergency.

When that was over, I was taken to the Governor's office. Major Harvey wore a tweed suit, and we went over to his house, where I met his wife. They had one daughter, Valery, at school. Much later on, my cousin Maurice married her; he was still in the Marines at this time.

I learned that the prison was built by, and for, the French Revolutionaries in the eighteenth century and continued to be the hardest prison to escape from, for long-term prisoners. The Major asked me whether I would like to go over some of it, and what interested me. I said, "The sick wards." So we walked through parts of the prison. I asked if I could speak to the patients. They all seemed very pleased and told me of their families and so on. The Major told me about the hardships of the staff and governors, and the responsibilities of the life. I knew it was not going to be a bed of roses.

H.M. Prison, Aylesbury

I passed my medical and was to report to H.M. Prison, Aylesbury, Bucks. The Governor, Miss Joan Martyn, came and met me at the gate. She showed me her office on the right-hand side and said, "I think we will go to my house and we'll get some tea." We returned back to the outside world and adjacent to the left side was a sizeable house.

Joan Martyn had been at Aylesbury for some time under Miss Bruce, whose grandfather was the Lord Melbourne and whose name graces the capital of Victoria, Australia. I was told the aims and differences of the Borstal System — the training of girls 16-20 years, who were in Wings A, B, and C, equivalent to houses. The prisoners were Stars, and were in the main part of the prison. They had not had previous convictions, but were in for murder, manslaughter, burglary, and very clever fraudulence, serving either long or life sentences. They were all screened from the courts into the London Holloway Prison, and "suitably" allocated to Aylesbury.

The Governor dealt with the prisoners through the Chief and Principal Officers. The remaining officers were in uniform and were on duty for prisoners and Borstal girls, who were not allowed to mix socially or at work. Some officers specialised in laundry work with large machines, cooking, farming and cleaning.

Joan Martyn ran a tight ship, but was approachable at all times by the staff. The prisoners had to book through the Principal Officer to see the Governor, and the girls through an officer or straight to the Housemistress; the girls often caught me in a corridor, usually with a triviality that I could deal with without bothering the Governor. Soon after I joined, we were to change our titles to Assistant Governors.

We wore mufti, but I found my officer's overcoat warm and beautifully tailored; it could be easily converted to an ordinary coat by exchanging the brass buttons for a deep grey and removing the shoulder tabs with the ranks on. I had my coat for many years.

The building that housed senior officers was ugly and gaunt. There were two bathrooms to each floor. I had a sitting room with a small bedroom and gas fire. On the ground floor was a flat for the Deputy Governor. When she left to be head of a new Borstal in Kent, the position was termed the Acting Governor. A special officer was allocated to supervise the cleaning of the rooms daily by the prisoners. There was a decent-sized pantry where we could wash our crockery. Downstairs was an unused large sitting room; there was a very large kitchen with ample space, and gas rings in each pantry to make pots of tea. The Prison was on a bus route, Aylesbury to Leighton Buzzard; we were a good mile from the town itself, but less than half a mile away was a splendid grocer who would deliver on certain days.

Market days were every Saturday; the stalls were all set up and we found the owners were usually doing a circuit from London. Everything was sold from pots and pans, fruit stalls, clothing, bolts of cloth, and even boots and shoes. The Housemistresses and the Chief Officer used to take selected girls, two to four, to go shopping for the staff. It was one way to teach trust.

The Assistant Governor attended the Governor's meeting every day at 9a.m. except Saturdays and Sundays. Each of us arranged our duties ourselves. We all worked alternate weekends.

All newspapers for the prisoners were censored — partly in fairness to a present transferred prisoner whose case was discussed in the press. There was pressure on all staff. One's room was always locked and no one could leave newspapers about in one's room during the day/morning when it was being cleaned; in fact we rigidly locked up our cupboards and writing materials which were much sought after.

After the Governor's meeting, we inspected our girls' Wing rooms and visited the sick in our small hospital; it was a normal average to have about eight or nine babies. There was one doctor and a local town doctor for a relief, four registered sisters, and one nurse. Prisoner patients were rare, but we had a 4-6-bed ward. We only had 30 women.

It was a dreadful time to be coping with the Borstal girls who had wandered the streets during the war; some were gypsies who had no schooling, some were orphans, and hardly any could read or write. That had not been tackled seriously, so it came to be my task.

We taught the girls after their mid-day meal, from 12.30 to 2p.m. I taught a class who could read and write, either history or English literature.

Another of the staff taught sewing and craftwork. With leave on roster, that left three or four of us. I prepared my class-work in the afternoon after a snatched lunch in my room. We had an excellent Public Library where we could order recent textbooks. As a respite from work, I enrolled in the County of Bucks education weekend courses. I attended Waterperry Horticulture College, which had, and still has, an excellent record for its exhibits in the Chelsea Flower Show. So I was able to cover their pruning of fruit trees, though naturally I had to be lucky for my weekend off to coincide with the course.

I should say that I saw at least six or seven people leaving, either to open up another institution or get married, or because the work was too exacting in as much as there were few hours off. We each did a round of the entire conglomerate of buildings, the equivalent to the work of Duty Officer. You made your own time after 11p.m. to walk to the stations of the night officers, because it was important they were safe and well, or might wish to report an incident. Of course, we were always at the end of a phone. It used to feel eerie when the moon shone through the panes of glass on the top floor in the main prison.

Prisons were planned in the shape of a cross; the centre core were posts of work and observance. Officers had one advantage of being in uniform, thus having a belt so you could hook your keys to a safety ring. Those keys weighted three and a half pounds. We Assistant Governors were in suits or blouse and skirt, all carrying keys; I usually wore a suit and under my jacket I had a belt to put my keys. Inmates have been known, especially in male institutions, to snatch keys and run. You can have more rapport with a person out of uniform, with no sight of keys. I found a human plus: the girls in my wing or house were intensely loyal, so if one or two inmates tried to be awkward or violent, it was amazing how the others bustled them away.

What was very tiring was that after their evening meal, we had to control a recreational hour. Sometimes we played games, most nights they listened to records. There were no funds for them, so we had to fork out money to buy a record quite often. Near Christmastime we were able to put on plays or a concert. When I was awake at night, I was able to plot a story to keep them amused for 20 minutes after a record. On some rare weekends I would see a film with James Floyd and I was often asked for every detail. I saw James in London and more rarely in Cuckfield.

In the summer, outside our quarters and the main wall were allotments of which only a few were taken up. So eventually I rented four adjacent plots; they were not big. I grew mostly flowers for the Chapel, salads,

271

herbs and strawberries. There were weekends when I stayed in the quarters to catch up with the usual personal chores. If Peggy Mason, the Principal Officer, was free we occasionally had a meal out in a country pub. Being on a good bus route, we had a choice of villages to explore. Otherwise I rested or slept. Sometimes, if it fitted in, I might stay in Cuckfield with James Floyd.

Routine

We had a magistrates' meeting every month where the governor gave her report on numbers of inmates, discharges, entrants and the present conditions. One branch, which was vital, was the probation officer's work. All girls were given a chance of work, often away from a home environment, so they could make a new start.

The most difficult cases were those whose babies were born in prison; a high proportion had syphilis or gonorrhea. It was a great sadness to see their babies with their eyes all messed up. The doctor and nurses were incredible; they were the old-fashioned kind and seemed inured to it. Although two years was the term of correction, those who were pregnant were released as soon as mother and child were able to go to a home. For a long while they were in the Probation Officer's care, or a member of the Borstal Welfare Office. They were sent out with a fixed amount of cash, a place to live and eventually work. It was a thankless task for some of the welfare people.

Miss Martyn always said even if one person made good it was rewarding; usual statistics showed over 37 per cent. I went on several courses. One was at

Cambridge at Clare College. One or two women usually attended a Governor's course, and the rest were about 24 male governors. We visited several industries from which the prisoner's environment at work could be understood. Another course was at Wakefield Prison, where all prison officers had their initial training. Wakefield town was the dreariest of industrialised cities. One of our field days was going over a coal-mine and all its aspects. The medical officer said I was not fit to go. The Senior Medical Officer eventually sent me to bed; he said I was suffering from post-war exhaustion and I had landed in another situation of one of the hardest jobs to deal with.

The prison industry as a whole was almost self supportive. Each prison had its own products; all our women's frocks were made in one female prison. Aylesbury's farm fully supplied all our milk with a Jersey herd, and all our green vegetables, cabbages, cauliflowers and salads, carrots and so on.

With the keenness of the Prison Commissioners' dedication to improve prisons and give scope for new ideas, the open prisons were being launched, at the beginning for first offenders and model, non-violent inmates. Aston Grange, near York, was the first women's Open Prison. It was a great success. It was a large house in extensive grounds, run like a practical college. After settling in, some prisoners took themselves off in the public bus to York to wander round the city. They were to be back by early evening; they had their work wages to spend and an allowance for lunch and tea.

I visited Cuckfield more often when the weather was good. James was much older; he had been in and out of hospital. He concentrated a great deal on his natural history notes and drawings of birds, insects, visits to the Zoological meetings and travelling to see his relatives in Scotland.

Coronation, 2 June, 1953

For the Coronation I received chair accommodation, reserved, in the Queen Victoria Memorial Area for my mother and myself. This came with plenty of advice — eight paragraphs. We were to be in position by 7.30a.m.

I was able to get accommodation in the quarters for mother; people were so very helpful. I am not sure how everything fell into place as I had influenza, most virulent. The Harrow friends helped; Helen's brother came every day and gave me the new penicillin injections. I knew I was just fit enough to take off in a hired car at 6a.m. We sat on tiered seats and we thought we had the best places as we could see the beginning of the procession coming out of the Palace gates. Before the procession, the police and the guards lined the crowds and the front of the stands. Loudspeakers relayed a lot of military tunes. We had to wait some time.

The spectacle was brilliant but I found the crowds overwhelming. The Queen looked radiant and the Duke looked fine. It was full pageantry on a grand, sunny day. The next day a registered package came with the Coronation Medal.

Change of Work, Not Location

I literally found everything hard work, and felt pretty ill and run down. I found I had a series of lumps; they were hard and aching. The local doctor was puzzled and could not give me any explanation. I landed in the Royal Bucks General Hospital in Aylesbury. I was barely seven stone and for six weeks I was a guinea pig for tests, which were sent to Stoke Manderville. I was in a 26-bed ward, and during the day I was wheeled out on to a balcony. A new surgeon arrived, very young, from Rangoon, just demobbed, and was made a resident doctor. He guessed at once what I had. A specialist sent me home to rest for six months, or more, after all the lumps were removed. The Civil Service had to send me to Harley Street on and off; each time I was unfit for Assistant Governor work. They offered me a Clerical Officer's job; in fact at Aylesbury the Discipline Clerk had retired. She had her own office, did all the Governor's letters and kept all the prisoners' records. I was in an ironical situation, but financially I had no option. I was allowed to keep my room and pay the same, including my allotments. I attended to the magistrates' needs and had every weekend off. I swallowed my pride during my first week. I was welcomed back as if nothing had happened, except I was in another office. It was hard, but I got better.

One of the magistrates was Lady Barlow, who was a professional botanist and a great gardener; she stayed on the Falkland Islands and collected plants for the first monograph on that area's botany. She always came to see me for a chat and I used to give her some plants she might like. She was to play a part in my future. Peggy Mason and I used to go out on several occasions. Her sister lived at Brighton, so she went there about once a month, and I occasionally went with her.

Death of an Old Friend

I had a painful note from Cuckfield. James Floyd was found dead from a heart attack in bed. The writer was an ex-serviceman he had employed when Claude left to go to Wales; he was looking after the animals and helping generally. He took himself off to an Army Officer who knew James well, returning they found the bedroom window open, but James died alone. That was a shock. I attended his funeral with neighbouring family friends. Later I found he had left me an inheritance, enough for me to leave the prison in my own time. There were a lot of things to clear up, and in fact it took a year.

Lady Barlow asked me if I would like to be interviewed by the Director of the Royal Botanic Gardens, Kew, for a position. I was most grateful. It would be so near London if I were considered. Sir Edward Salisbury took me round a great deal of the gardens and asked me what I knew about certain plants. He seemed to be satisfied I had a general knowledge of plant life. He had checked that I had collected Cornish plants, which were in the Herbarium.

I was told I would hear in a week's time; I gathered he would be seeing where vacancies might occur. Later I was asked to attend an interview with Dr. Turrill, the Keeper of the Herbarium, who needed an assistant; there was quite a variety of work both inside and out. I was very happy. I stayed a few nights at the Priory Hotel quite cheaply whilst I found a bed-sit. The money was good. I could live on it whilst I was arranging all the matters with James' relatives and solicitors.

Alec Beecham was upset with me because I said I could not marry him as I was not in love with him, but I respected him as a good friend. He very soon found an amenable widow and settled in Falmouth. He continued to visit my mother.

Working at Kew Gardens

There were some family hiccups over James's inheritance, so those were settled with the help of my cousins in Kensington. I just felt a deep loss of a great, much older and beloved friend. We had so much in common, he was a wonderful teacher, gentle and kind, and full of surprises.

On 30 May 1955 Miss Mellanby wrote from the Prison Commission, which touched me deeply:

Dear Daphne, I longed to stop the car last Tuesday evening, but Mr. Storr was in a great state about driving in the dark. I was in two minds whether to write to you when I heard the news of your legacy, but somehow it seemed rather cold-blooded to congratulate you on a piece of good fortune, which also involved the death of a very old friend. However, now that you have left us I do in the first place want to say how very sorry I am about that. Although you would of course be mad to do anything else, I was always delighted that it was possible for you to stay in another capacity, even though your health was not up to the strenuous housemistress job, and we had been very fortunate to keep you so long. Miss Mason particularly will miss you badly, but so will everyone else.

I do hope you are going to be able not merely to live comfortably, but to do exciting things with this windfall. Not aerial photography, perhaps, but at least start some interesting travel. You have had a long struggle to carry out your domestic responsibilities, I know, and it is wonderful to feel that burden is permanently lifted. I do wish I had seen you to say goodbye. But this is just to send you my regret that we have lost you, my best wishes for a happy time ahead. Yours sincerely, M. Mellanby.

That letter is still treasured. I must add that we met again in about six or seven years' time in another country and was I able to help her in her task with a car and take her to picnics, and to prisons, which was the purpose of the journey.

I was a breadwinner again, without much worry, and could afford many useful extras. Of course there is always a challenge.

New Idea

I walked all the roads in the vicinity of Kew Gardens, trying to work out an idea that sprang up at work. There was no nursery for plants among the few shops adjacent to the Coach and Horses public house or at the other end of the main garden entrance at Kew. Lying at the back of the Coach and Horses was a road which contained a rectangular site which years ago had been a nursery. It had an underground air-raid shelter and collapsed tangle of a greenhouse, with an old grape vine weaving in and out of brickwork and weeds. A chapel had been built in a small wedge opening on the road and very much in use, but behind it was unused land with old fruit trees and another greenhouse.

The owner, an elderly woman called Dolly, who lived opposite, was poor and earned a bit by buying fruit and potatoes from the market and selling them cheaply, and doing odd jobs. I asked her if she ever thought of selling it. "No," she said, "lots of people want it for building." I tested the waters, so to speak, in the Herbarium: "Do you think there is a need for hardy, unusual plants, seen in Kew Gardens, including a rose nursery?" Several botanists said there would be staff support, and most likely also support from the locals.

283

First, I had to have a house to live in, get it modernised, and find a team to clear the old nursery — if I could get the title. Luckily the land was registered as a nursery or for agricultural use. Dolly agreed to sell. My lawyer was in Aylesbury, so I called on the Barclay's Bank manager, who was just over the river next to the market. I had transferred James Floyd's account to them. I then discussed my plans with my cousins. They were very business-like, helped me store furniture, and dealt with difficulties with great firmness.

Eventually, and quickly, I bought the little house in Gloucester Road, which was up for sale, and set the local builder, who lived in the same road, to do the few alterations and the painting. New flashing in the roof was needed. I put in an Aga boiler for heating the house and bath-rails. Kew could be very damp: only one row of houses lay between the Thames and us. I was recommended an architect who had modern techniques for shop reconstruction, colours and designs. My great concern was to rescue the grape vines. I learned that the gardener who planted Hampton Court's famous 200-year-old vine lived off Kew Green and cultivated vines. I got it confirmed that this tangled mess was the same variety as at Hampton. So there was a retail shop with storerooms, and new sand-block heating which was boosted by electricity.

I had offers from young overseas botanists who were keen to work weekends. They were glad of the money coming in, as they were on grants. I began with two at first. There was a very high wall at right angles to the roadway, which was the back of the broken glass-house.

This wall was in good condition; a new kind of glass, curved, was built up to the wall from a parallel low existing one. Lengths of unbroken vine were carefully tied together, whilst all the broken glass was gathered in containers. On Mondays, a rubbish man carted stuff away, prunings, weeds, the lot. Then the fellows dug and forked all the beds between sparsely scattered apple trees; cinder paths were uncovered, remade and edged.

One botanist had a mother who had to leave her work at a place nearby. She was trained in bookkeeping so I employed her for one and a half hours a week until we were stocked, then she worked full time. Whilst I was at work, the rubbish man had to be paid and progress made on the house; there was a list of things to be purchased, including thick gloves and worktools. I never had a phone in the house as I was rarely there, but I had one booked for our future shop with an extension to the first building — a concrete room with skylights and a large window — called "the Studio". Eventually I had to house all James' paintings which were later exhibited at Wilton's Gallery, London, we sold 50 per cent; it was by invitation only. The shop was cleverly designed to include the air-raid shelter. Richmond Council would not rescind its law — "No removal of built air-raid shelters" — so we turned it into a horticultural tools and sundries section, but it was a nuisance, with not much width. Later I appealed again to have one wall inside halved, but again received a firm refusal.

All the new materials were used and had completed their trials; everything was fireproof. We completed everything in six months. The gardener from South Middlesex Hospital came on Saturdays and Sundays and shaped and pruned the vine, and set it up in its newly shaped glass home. He gave me instructions, as well as teaching me all the time, and he agreed to visit to spray and prune in the right seasons. He had been in charge of vines for years. In the future we grew and sold standard fuchsias, geraniums and heliotropes in large pots in the Vine House — a late Victorian craze which we began again.

Herbarium Routine

My work at the Herbarium, from 9a.m. to 4p.m., was gathering momentum. When Dr. Turrill was away in the Balkans (his area), he sent batches of pressed plants that had to be fumigated and processed. When my boss was back I was immersed in proof reading. At that time all serious works were written in Latin so that anyone in the botanic world could study and read them. He and I sat at the long table in his office; every 45 minutes we stretched our legs. His famous books on liliums were published with drawings and paintings by Margaret Stones, born in Australia, who was a brilliant artist. Dr. Turrill gave her guidelines for professional botanical painting, a special skill.

The house which contained the Herbarium specimens, the dried and labelled plants, was George III's own house. The original stairs, which were carefully edged with lead to preserve the wood, are still there. The front part on the first floor holds the small but wonderful library; this is frequently used by the staff and visiting botanists from all over the world. The new part added to the back has circular stairs going up to each floor. The ground floor has the famous Index Kewensis. An assistant is especially trained to help those who visit to get the hang of the system. Each family of plants had a number and location.

Heavy metal slide doors were used to enter each floor, because fire would be a disaster: all the cupboards containing the folders were wooden. There were many bays, each bay with a long table on which to study the flowers, or label and write.

Plant Nursery and Retail Work

The summer time was wonderful — the long hours were much appreciated, so I could continue work at the nursery. I called it "Hanover Nursery". Inside the shop the walls were a delicate shade colour to reflect the fruits and plant colours; we had two shop windows. Our fruit and vegetables were in round baskets of fine cane, in three sizes. A door from the shop opened into our glass-house full of flowering plants under the vine, and on through to the outside nursery with its lines of bedding plants and seedlings. A low-level greenhouse near the studio had a crop of lettuces and early tomatoes. In the newly built greenhouse, after the first season the grape vine began flowering: to our great joy from then onwards it yielded magnificent crops.

Mrs. O'Brien, our book-keeper, was very strict, watching customers to see they were served, and was excellent in balancing the accounts, checking order books, seeing that there was plenty of change in the till. We had a full-time foreman, also a trained gardener selling outside, and inside a full-time saleswoman, Mrs. Lovell, who lived nearby. She was a trained florist, so

289

she and her husband often worked on wreaths and bouquets at night. They were on a percentage basis and chose what they required through Mrs. O'Brien, who went to the market in our re-painted green van with Mr. Smee who was a night lock-keeper higher up on the Thames. He "did" the market and deliveries. I went once a week irregularly and noted newcomers and quality; the market opened at 5a.m. We dealt with the best produce dealers who were paid personally by Mrs. O'Brien on Thursdays. Sometimes I had a schoolboy who ran errands for local deliveries. I should mention that Dolly, the previous owner, used to help and clean. We also, in peak season, took on known "casuals", such as a doctor's wife, for the mornings. They told their friends, which helped build up clientele, and also gave a good input of suggestions. We had a florist's room with a large sink and benches, also a small, well equipped kitchen with chairs. The till was behind a tinted trellis, which had a well-equipped corner for books and a telephone nook.

After our first year of trading we made 25 per cent profit. I did not have a salary but used damaged fruit and vegetables free. The staff bought items at cost, and if customers had bulk items they were given a discount. We had a fine selection of honeys, exotic fruits, chutneys, and several pickles of quality. Two hives of bees under the apple trees added interest; the beekeeper had quite a few in the outer London suburbs.

One day in the Herbarium, Dr. Melville, head of the Australasian Department, sent for me and said that

290

when he was in Australia, he was given an assistant from Melbourne Botanic Gardens. Her name was Mervyn Davis and she had completed her Landscape Course at Durham University. She was looking for work whilst she did her final thesis. "Could you employ her?" he asked me. I said I would discuss it with Mrs. O'Brien. Her son was the botanist who was working on grasses in the Herbarium. I had to see this young woman about her hours. She had been through Burnley Horticultural College in Melbourne, which was well known.

Another Australian Arrives

My mother was staying with me on a visit. We had three bedrooms and there was plenty of room, but I decided our new Australian would lodge out because of cooking, etc. There was a very nice person, a widow, who sometimes took in botanists on their visits. So it was arranged for Mervyn Davis to come over on Sunday for tea, to see her room and the nursery. I do remember it was one of those dreary, dull days which make Gloucester Road look such a backwater. At home a fire was sparkling, we were now on anthracite — all heating was designed accordingly. Mother had made some scones. It was suggested that before it rained we should go along to meet the landlady, which we did. Everything was clean, but rather cheerless; the new linoleum did not help. Mervyn smiled politely.

When we returned and made tea, Mervyn asked if she could stay with me as it was much more homely. I agreed, as Mervyn was a very cheerful, solid person, adaptable and a good cook.

We had sold the Cornish cottage at St Agnes and bought another Coastguard cottage in Sennen Cove; it was almost on the beach next to the Lifeboat house and launching ramp. The downstairs kitchen, dining room and entrance hall were red-tiled and polished. Upstairs were three and a half rooms, and a spacious living room. Mother chose some new curtains. Her friends from Penzance could come and see her, as there was a reasonable bus service. The views were magnificent to Cape Cornwall. Whilst in Kew, mother had news that her sister Edith, who had moved to a farm at North Ilminster, Somerset, had died. We both went down and booked into an Ilminster Hotel. I was able to arrange the funeral at Weymouth, where Aunt Edith was cremated. None of my cousins could come; Uncle George was executor and her solicitor, but could not attend either. However he gave me masses of instructions and I had to do all the paper work. This delayed Mervyn from coming for a week or so.

The young farm couple were very helpful; apparently my aunt had been treated for cancer for some time; we did not know that. In a few days we returned to Kew and soon my mother returned to Sennen Cove.

Robbery

One very foggy day I returned to Gloucester Road and found my front door broken into, as if someone had used a hammer, the entire paneling was smashed. I walked around in utter disbelief — all my books were pulled out on to the floor and drawers from the desk tipped out. I walked into the kitchen, and on the table was the Georgian teapot ready to be cleaned, untouched. A small sum of money was left, ready to pay the milkman. Cutlery drawers and cupboards were just left open. I went across the road and round into the shop and phoned the police. The staff had not heard anything. I returned and the police arrived; a Sergeant Carter was in charge. I told him I had not been upstairs. My bedroom was ransacked, all the drawers tipped out, bedding tipped over. The front room was unoccupied, just the bedding strewn about, the same with the back room. Mervyn Davis fortunately had not yet arrived.

I turned up the Aga to hot, as I could not get the front door fixed. I think someone got a few boards and hessian to keep the cold out a bit. So the result: my cameras gone, some innocuous papers had been gone through; I found a lot of films gone and all the Russian correspondence (vetted by Air Ministry) stolen. Then I felt a terrible fear — it was not a common thief: a purse in a drawer was untouched and all the silver. I made some tea, and I gave my fingerprints to the man checking around. Sergeant Carter rang the Police Station in Richmond to say he was about to be off-duty and he would stay the evening until early morning and could someone relieve him. Incidentally my guns were still in the hall cupboard untouched, which was amazing, also the ammunition I kept upstairs.

I thought I ought to get a meal together. I cooked some steak, as all the food was untouched. Mrs. O'Brien had rung the builder, who would fit a new door in the morning. I shuddered, the awful feeling that the unknown was still around. Dick Carter was putting the books back in the shelves. I went up and made my bed up and tried to get the room in order, but I was shocked and very afraid — like shadows unseen but felt.

At 10p.m. two police cars arrived and a conference was swiftly held. The terrible rail crash at Lewisham had happened and every spare policeman had been told to report, so one car with one man would patrol an extra round and Dick Carter had to leave. I believe 40 people were killed in the head-on crash. The Carters became friends of mine, in due course; at first his wife or a policeman would give us a reassuring call to the shop in the morning.

Arising from our plant orders, I was asked to look at gardens to see where the plants should be placed. Around Kew Green there were Georgian houses with balanced sized gardens, usually walled in. They were well established and the owners, especially new owners, sometimes decided to remove a big tree to let the light in and replace it with a modest shrub. These were pleasant visits and I was getting new customers for our other goods.

We had monthly lists from established wholesale nurseries, so if the customer chose to wait we could get what he or she wanted. If they lived locally, Jack, the foreman, could plant trees and shrubs for them.

We had a set of representatives visiting; I was a member of the Farmers' Union, whose journal had an excellent horticultural section. I attended a few of their meetings, especially their annual one which had trade exhibitions and lectures. The one I enjoyed most was in Edinburgh for three days. We were only an embryo nursery, but selling quality fruit and vegetables carried us through the bad-weather months. A lot of plants were heeled in; Jack did a quantity of grafted roses in rows at the rear end, in good light.

When Mervyn Davis arrived she was interested in the gardening side. The Australian technical side of treating some plants was completely different; the climates in Australia altered their time of flowering and treatment. We had to iron out that problem. She was extremely useful at window-dressing with plants and horticultural sundries, which I had done, and that gave me an extra two or three hours a week. Also she tackled the very small, dull front and back gardens of Gloucester Road, which was very rewarding.

Naturally we had our differences; she had been studying plans for large areas for factories and municipalities. Her private work at home was in all types of domestic gardens that could grow tender plants, which in England would only thrive in some parts of Cornwall and greenhouses. I bought a tri-car, with three wheels, so she could go and study customers' needs and help get us about quickly.

The Victoria Cross and George Cross Association

In 1958 Mervyn took me to my first Victoria Cross and George Cross Association meeting in Regent Street. I was dropped off opposite the Café Royal where we were to meet. Mervyn said she saw me standing on the island in the street, quite petrified to cross the road; she thought I did not look like a George Cross winner. It is one of my great weaknesses, I still find crossing roads in traffic terrifying.

Brigadier Sir John Smyth, V.C., M.C., was approached by members of the Victoria Cross Reunion in the centenary year, suggesting that he should form a V.C. Association, and he became the first chairman. At the time Sir John was a busy Member of Parliament and the new association would have no headquarters or staff. The Royal Society of St George had particular connections with the Victoria Cross, and offered their boardroom at St George's House for meetings, which Sir John accepted. At their second meeting, it was suggested to invite holders of the George Cross, including the George Cross Island of Malta; this was enthusiastically accepted.

Her Majesty the Queen granted her Royal Patronage and Sir Winston Churchill agreed to become the first President. The George Cross holders were admitted to full membership. A Royal Warrant was signed and the Association was renamed "The Victoria Cross and George Cross Association". This first reunion was held at the Café Royal on 24 July 1958, when the General Meeting was held. The Guest of Honour was HRH the Duke of Gloucester; other guests included Mr. Duncan Sandys, Minister of Defence. Ninety VCs and thirty-nine GCs attended the dinner. At the end of 1959 there were 304 VCs living and 138 GCs. The notes and figures have been obtained from *The Story of the George Cross* by Brigadier The Rt. Hon. Sir John Smyth, Bt, VC, GC.

My copy of this book was autographed by the author, Jackie Smyth, VC; 27 GCs and Jean Gomme-Duncan, now Mrs. D. Inglefield. Her devotion to the Association did a tremendous job.

Jean, the Secretary

(This is a good time to bring up an action Jean Gomme-Duncan, the Secretary of the Victoria Cross and George Cross Association, took some years later, when her godfather said, "Now is the time to give you your legacy to carry out your longing to visit every VC and GC in their homes in so many countries." This she did, and investigated their needs in Central Africa, throughout Australia, New Zealand, Nepal, India, Pakistan, Middle East and Canada; she was intrepid and was the right person at the right time. It took ten months in all.)

My mother had written to say that the doctor had told her she should move away from having to climb hills to get to transport, and should begin to have care. Before, she told me she had contacted Admiral Tyrell's Housing Foundation, which started in Scotland when he turned his large home into flats or bed-sits for the elderly; he then founded other places. There was a vacancy at the Manor House in Dormansland near East Grinstead, so we went for a couple of nights, staying at Ye Dorset Arms; some Cornish friends called Broad owned a farm nearby and said it was a fabulous place; Mrs. Broad came with us to the Manor.

300

It was a very large house set in a woodland area, with a large garden and a lovely view. What was offered was the tower flat: you entered from the near staircase into a charming room with a turret bay so she had views of the south and west. There was a small bedroom, bathroom and kitchenette for limited cooking. Downstairs was a large dining room for lunches and dinners. There were quite a few couples who had their cars who could get about. But at the end of the drive there was a bus stop, a few cottages and a small inn called The Plough. One paid a large deposit down and so much percentage was deducted each year; and if one left, the balance was returned. The manager and his wife were ex-army and their management of the place was excellent. Keen gardeners were encouraged to help if they wished. There was a snag: there was no lift, but mother said it was nothing compared to the cliffs and hills she had been walking.

Mrs. Broad said there was an excellent doctor at East Grinstead. Mother was looking well but was sad at leaving Cornwall. So the move was decided. I put mother on the train at Reading to Penzance, where someone was meeting her there to go to Sennen. There was no shortage of people who wanted to buy the Coastguard house, it was in good condition to live in or to let, fully modernised. Eventually I moved her to Dormansland, with most of her furniture.

I had given my notice in to Kew Gardens altogether; I was paid under the Moxon Trust. My recent boss, Mr. Charles Hubbard, a grass expert, became the Keeper; he was a very good man, quiet, hard-working, and much respected. Dr. Turrell had retired. He was to be missed, as another team for the Balkans had to be found. The staff gathered in the tea break, wishing me well, and to my amazement gave me a large signed card with the Herbarium depicted on the front of a set of *Royal Horticultural Society Dictionary of Plants*. I was very touched. All the botanists' names are still there. I felt and feel now very humble; I was such a small cog in a very large wheel.

Whilst I was at the Nursery, Margaret Sims turned up. She had written from New Zealand about her engagement to Lewis Black, ex-POW. Now they had arrived in England and set up house at Compton Chase, overlooking Sussex. She wanted 300 attractive roses, all of a kind, to plant up the driveway. I suggested a new prize rose of the time, called Masquerade. I was lucky to get them delivered as they were scarce. When they were duly planted, someone came in at night and stole the lot. I could not get any more. So I shuffled round a collection of roses that ought to flower together the same weeks, and patterned them out in mixed batches. Apparently, plant stealing was rife at the time.

A while later Daphne Barnes phoned and we arranged for her and Kenneth to have tea with me on a Sunday. Kenneth had taken an apartment and an elderly relative organised the small household. Daphne B. was permanently in Cyprus, which I knew, because she was a great letter-writer. She described the politics, the life and the manual work and activities of the Cypriots. Much later than this she vividly described her life whilst the Turkish invasion was on, with the British mostly huddled on the beach waiting for the Royal Navy to evacuate them.

Peggy Mason used to come up for the odd weekend; her mother had died and she was looking after her sister Betty, who was at work, but not very strong. She corresponded with Joan Marytn and various staff who had retired from the Prison Service. They soon closed the Aylesbury Borstal and the women's prison down; it became an all-male prison in 1959.

Mervyn Davis left us to go home in time for Christmas 1958. She had done her Nottingham thesis, and she became a member of the International Federation of Landscape Architects, only conditional on Australia forming its own Institute and becoming a national member. She returned to her home, where her aunt lived who was now ill and sadly having to go into a home. Aunty Mundall was a war widow, her husband survived Gallipoli, he was one of the last to leave, but was sent to France. He later took some Allied officers round the Front and a sniper shot him not long before the armistice was signed. Mervyn's eldest sister was married with three children and lived near the Royal Botanic Gardens.

Hanover Nursery is Sold

I was getting very tired and under the weather, with the fogs and damp of the Thames. My doctor lived near us and said the cold and wet weren't doing me any good. She mentioned that she was giving up her practice and going to Brisbane with her husband, who was going on some expedition (Hall's) under the auspices of the British Museum (Natural History). She would continue working as a doctor. I told her I was discussing things with my cousins in Kensington: whilst the nursery was at its peak, it would be time to sell. The foreman Jack was leaving for a job near his home with fewer hours. Mervyn had invited me to Australia for six months. She had not been able to get work as a Landscape Architect (quite a new profession for Australia) and thought she would set up privately. She had a father and stepmother in another suburb.

I told the staff I was putting the nursery up for sale and relied on them to see me through this; so I put it in the hands of Hampton auctioneers and Aylesbury solicitors. The board went up: Hanover Nursery and Retail Shop, Cambridge Road, Kew, freehold and vacant possession. Mrs. O'Brien said she would tide me over, but she was getting older and used to our routine and she would retire. She made good suggestions about the closing. We would be showing people around. I felt defeated but hoped I had built up something worthwhile.

I had made friends with a family on Kew Green associated with BOAC. I had written up some articles on horticultural history in relation to plants, people and places. I had made friends with a Swiss wife and husband who asked me to help them make a rose garden in Putney. Eric was the London editor of a Swiss press agency of French and German magazines, and his wife Renée was a brilliant cook and a good businesswoman in jewellery. I told them about the nursery and that I was going to Australia. Eric said, "Go on the inaugural flight of the New Comet 4. I will give you a Press Card, write up the trip; the passengers will all be journalists and a politician or two. When you are in Australia try and interview as many Swiss migrants as you can about their way of living and what they do." My Kew Green friends arranged for me to go over BOAC at Heathrow, the food, kitchens, over the Comet 4, so I had the "gen" on the project before the flight.

There were very, many weeks ahead. I sold the little house in Gloucester Road easily; it was freehold, modernised and an elderly mother and daughter had the money and were ready to move in to suit me. I saw many people who wanted the nursery site for other things, but Richmond Council refused to rescind the law in regard to the wretched air-raid shelter. They began digging up the road to put new pipes and drainage pits in. The neighbours were appalled, and so was I, at how the huge vine roots had attacked everything under the pavements and asphalt. I thought I was in trouble but they had been negligent over drainage, and I sought advice and got another large pit put in. It filtered through my mind that it was the Vine's revenge. The sale was in London at Hampton's; quite a lot of people were there, but many questioned the auctioneer over the shelter. The price was half its value because of the shelter. Then one man hung on with small bids. I shook my head. The man was taken aside and he said he was a nurseryman with his wife. I had shown them over before. He came from Suffolk, and was a nephew of the builder in our road. I was not impressed but he said he could pay the first deposit and the remainder in two or three parts. He produced the first cheque, but I did not trust him or the situation. I asked him where he was registered as a nurseryman. He vaguely said Suffolk. But I checked all the lists and he was not on them. Hampton's said to me, "You have no choice, we cannot get anywhere with Richmond Council." I packed up all my things including the studio pictures and some tools which I use today; we were agents for Wilkinson Sword Company and many others, so I took complete sets. I did not lose any money but I did not make any fortune; I made a lot of good friends, and financially I gained in experience.

Anyway, the Suffolk people came and the first thing was they announced they did not need any staff. They actually moved in the back of the shop with two children. I thought the Council would not tolerate that. I worried about who was going to look after the vine; it had been reaching its peak of fruiting, and customers had even booked their bunches, which had been carefully thinned to give the fruit its perfect shape. It was a miracle, but with much care and thought, it had been restored for 10 years or more. Who was carefully going to cut the bunches without them losing their bloom, handing each bunch down to each box with its white soft padding, held by another helper. They were sold for the table without blemish and fetched a good price. We harvested the last crop and were very satisfied. I asked Fortnum and Mason where they got their boxes from.

I went over to Dormansland for two nights; my mother had already made some friends. The good thing was the residents could ask the management about lunches or dinners for their friends. There were spare tables for extra people. The time would come to say goodbye, but she knew she would see me for certain when the VC and GC Association had their reunion each year. But I was only going for six months!

I made friends with the landlord of The Plough and his good lady. He was a retired Superintendent of Police; his wife Hilda was a very good organiser, and they had two rooms extra for bed and breakfast. He also had a spare garage. I was driving a small, standard estate car so Mr. Farnham agreed that when I went away I could have the end garage. He would give the car a run now and again.

Mother was staying a few days at Ye Dorset Arms, East Grinstead. I stayed a night with her and left the car at The Plough. Mrs. Broad's daughter Gwen drove me to the nearest junction to catch the train to London.

I cannot remember where I actually slept on my last night. I had said goodbye to the Riddells, the Stephens, Miss Blake, the Swayne Thomases and the Wigets. Alex, who was Mrs. Lovell's husband, the very black-haired, smart gypsy, drove me to Heathrow. There was a great party there. Press photographer Hans was hovering, and an entourage of Indian Royalty attached themselves. I was overweight with luggage which was waived; customs enjoyed waving us through. Alex was dragged in for a drink; I was afraid he might be coming too! Heathrow was not large then. I seemed to be surrounded by various friends to see me off on Comet 4, Inaugural Flight 714, 1 November 1959, London to Sydney. First stop was Frankfurt, where I posted the first envelope to my mother. We were 11 minutes late in take-off.

We had a wonderful welcome in Singapore; the national city drink seemed to be Brandy Crusters. The rather small reception bar got very noisy and hot. Our next stop was Darwin, Australia, in the just-lighting-up dawn. We were given showers and breakfast and we walked around; outside I experienced the Northern Australian heat. It was in Darwin, that pleasant and leisurely place, that they examined our fingernails — apparently to make sure we had no "black" blood, which I did not realise at the time. Then through to

Brisbane, and Sydney, and the last stop for me, Melbourne.

As I walked across the tarmac at Essendon Airport, there were Mervyn and some friends I had met in London. They were all racegoers, and I spoiled their Melbourne Cup Day, 2 November 1959. The champagne flowed and the welcome was warm on that grey, cold day in Melbourne.

POSTSCRIPT

By Audrey Jarvis

The writings of Daphne Pearson extend to 1959. Unfortunately Daphne was unable to continue with the story of her life as she had planned. It was suggested that I present to the reader what is known of her subsequent life.

You have read that Daphne travelled to Australia on the inaugural flight of the BOAC Comet 4 on 1 November 1959. The trip was orchestrated by Dr. Eric Wiget, the London editor of a Swiss press agency of French and German magazines. Daphne had helped Dr. Wiget and his wife Renee establish a rose garden at their home in Putney, and subsequently wrote several articles for him. He arranged for her to be provided with a press pass, and her brief was to record the experience of the flight and the people she met.

In December 1959, soon after her arrival in Victoria, Daphne interviewed and photographed the noted author Nevil Shute Norway at his country home. He was an Englishman who made Australia his home. The best-selling British author at that time, he is probably best known for "A Town Like Alice", later made into a film. Daphne said she had no need to ask questions because he was eager to talk about Australia to an English newcomer. He told her he believed Australia to be the greatest country of the future, and that in 100 years' time its population would exceed 100 million. Nevil Shute died unexpectedly in January 1960 at the age of 60, just a few weeks after that interview.

In a letter to Daphne dated 31 December 1959, Dr. Wiget wrote:

> Another idea cropped up, to interview and take photographs of the Australian Prime Minister Menzies. That should not be too difficult. I met him once in London and was struck by his excellent Churchillian speech. I consider him as one of the most important of the Commonwealth Prime Ministers. Photographs and articles should give his importance and show him at home and perhaps in office as well.

History does not relate whether Daphne sought, or secured, this interview. In the same year Dr. Wiget put an interesting proposition to Daphne:

> There is another story which I think of interest — that is your life story. You could end it up or start with speaking about your trip and enter into the past. I know that Illustre, which comes out in French, would be most keen to publish it.

In the event this idea was put aside for many years.

Daphne was adjusting to life in a different part of the world and to the practicalities of finding employment. She had been invited to Australia by Mervyn Davis, her friend from Kew Garden days and a landscape

314

architect who had been studying in England. Mervyn's was a fledgling profession, particularly for women, in Australia at that time and finding work was difficult. Daphne helped her friend set up an office where Mervyn became established as a private consultant. Her career flourished with major works in landscape construction and development. She was a prime mover in the establishment in the mid-1960s of the Australian Institute of Landscape Architects, and its first woman Fellow.

Daphne's own working life in Australia led her into areas of great personal interest, particularly horticulture. During these early years she worked for the Department of Agriculture as well as helping Mervyn Davis in her landscape practice. Around this time her mother joined her to live in Australia. The lifestyle and climate in Australia suited Daphne well. She embarked on camping expeditions, exploring and discovering the bushland and flora of Victoria, so very different to that in England. She was able to pursue her interest in collecting specimens. Although in England she had been dogged by ill health, except for arthritis in later years her general health markedly improved in her adopted country.

In the late 1960s she joined the Commonwealth Department of Civil Aviation as a horticulturist for the Victoria and Tasmania regions. This job entailed coaxing the surrounds of the new Tullamarine (Melbourne) airport into gardens of international standard. The landscape architect for this undertaking was Mervyn Davis. They worked hard to establish the

315

plantings, creating beauty from the windswept landscape which had been farmland. It was felt that as Australia was usually at the end of a very long journey, travellers would welcome the sight of native eucalypt trees as well as beautiful roses and other exotics. So it proved to be. Daphne worked on the landscape at Launceston airport in Tasmania and later took over similar maintenance at Tullamarine, Launceston and Hobart airports. This was more than enough to challenge her. She compiled a manual to assist the staff with plant care.

With flying across Bass Strait a regular feature of her life, Daphne came to love Tasmania and its beauty. The south-west of the island is a land of jagged ranges, rain forest, raging rivers and rocky headlands. In the north of this area lie the wild Gordon and Franklin rivers, where a hydro-electric scheme was proposed in 1979. Feelings about the resultant destruction were fierce and community resentment was such that Dr. Bob Brown, now a Tasmanian parliamentarian, spearheaded the formation of the Tasmanian Wilderness Society. Yehudi Menuhin became its patron, and the effusive English botanist, Dr. David Bellamy, flew to Tasmania to lend support. He said: "This is one of the last true wilderness areas on earth where man truly has had no effect at all." Daphne was a practical support and with some 8,000 others wrote to the then Prime Minister, Malcolm Fraser, to express concern about the proposal. She also communicated with Dr. Brown. It was a bitter, long and hard-fought struggle which proved to be the greatest conservation campaign in

Australian history, but eventually the battle was won and this pristine wilderness area saved.

Bob Brown wrote to Daphne on 28 July 1984:

I am at long last feeling easy. Thank you again for your kindness at that frenetic time.

Daphne had retired in 1976 at the age of 65. She lived with Mervyn on a country property along the Old Sydney Road at Donnybrook, not far north of Melbourne. It was a peaceful place with expansive views. In collaboration with the noted botanist Dr. Jim Willis, with Mervyn Davis and Dr. J. W. Green of Western Australia, she began work on a bibliography of collectors and illustrators of Australian plants from the 1780s to the 1980s. More than 2,000 names were collated, and this pioneering work is now held in the National Herbarium at the Royal Botanic Gardens, Melbourne. Daphne loved books; she delved, researched and recorded meticulously. This passion stayed with her for the rest of her life.

In 1958, the year before moving to Australia, she had attended the inaugural meeting and reunion of the Victoria Cross and George Cross Association. This organisation went from strength to strength. Abiding friendships were made, and the association became an important part of Daphne's life, even from Australia. Reunions were held annually between 1961-68, and then in alternate years. Daphne attended with Mervyn as her guest. As the association is under Royal patronage — the Queen is its patron, and the Queen

Mother its president — reunions involve a church service attended by the Queen Mother, afternoon tea at St James' Palace, and receptions every third year at Buckingham Palace.

Daphne's attendance in the early 1980s was affected by Mervyn Davis's protracted illness. Daphne supported Mervyn, who had been awarded the MBE in 1980, with unswerving dedication until her death in 1985. It was a difficult time, but she was encouraged by friends and members of the Victoria Cross and George Cross Association to attend the 1986 reunion. Early that year I had met Daphne, and was invited to accompany her to London to assist her. An enduring friendship was born.

In May 1995, holders of the Victoria Cross and of the wartime George Cross were an integral part of the ceremonies in Hyde Park that commemorated the 50th anniversary of the victory in Europe. The Queen Mother attended these ceremonies, and afterwards met the holders of these illustrious awards — by now relatively few in number given the passage of years. The next day the English daily newspapers carried prominently located photographs of Daphne being presented to the Queen Mother, with a short account of the circumstances of her award.

Quickly there came a phone call from Scotland. The next week Daphne was flown by jet to Aberdeen Airport by Mr. Stephen Bond of Bond Helicopters Ltd., then transported by helicopter to the picturesque area of Deeside for lunch at Raemoir House Hotel, Banchory. This occasion was of vital import to the

Bond family. Although they had never met Daphne, the newspaper photograph had identified her to them as the woman who had rescued their father, Pilot Officer David Bond, from the fateful crash of his bomber 55 years earlier.

David Bond married after the war, and had four sons. Five members of the Bond family were present for that celebratory lunch. Daphne described it later as a wonderful, memorable day. "Meeting the family was so special," she said. I was privileged to share in the day. I remember that we saw snow falling amongst clumps of daffodils, and that we were back in our hotel in London at 8p.m.!

Daphne was present in 1997 at the Imperial War Museum, London, when Prince Charles opened the newly established Victoria Cross and George Cross Room. Awards bequeathed to the nation — which now include Daphne's own George Cross and service medals — now had a permanent home. Of particular significance was that the memorable portrait of Daphne that had been painted by Dame Laura Knight during the war also had a permanent home. It is a strong painting that evokes tenacity and courage as well as sensitivity. It was a fitting tribute to Daphne as this was to be her last visit to Great Britain.

In Australia during her retirement Daphne was invited to share in the Anzac Day and Remembrance Day services at the Australian War Memorial in Canberra. I went with her on these occasions. We were present on 11 November 1993 at the poignant funeral service for the Unknown Australian Soldier from the

First World War, brought home from France. She was made a life member of the Royal Air Force Association — Melbourne branch, and of the Women's Royal Air Force Association in the United Kingdom.

Daphne had continued to live in the country, but the location was too remote. In January 1989 at the age of 78, she moved to the Melbourne suburb of Canterbury to be closer to friends and medical facilities. Throughout her life, wherever Daphne landed she had the happy knack of getting to know people with her warmth of personality and her twinkling smile. She had a great ability to make and keep friends of all ages and from all walks of life. Her correspondence was constant and the postman was an integral part of her life as she maintained contact with friends in England. While many of her relatives had died she wrote regularly to her cousin, Lady Lorna Anderson, in Dumbartonshire, who is known for her feats in climbing and love of art. A long-established and oft-mentioned friend was Margaret Black, a cipher officer in the war years. She was a frequent visitor to Australia and a great support to Daphne. After Margaret died, members of her family living in Melbourne continued this support.

In February 2000 Mrs. Didy Grahame, secretary of the Victoria Cross and George Cross Association, came to Australia and visited Daphne. They knew each other well, and despite the fact that Daphne was in poor health, they spent valuable time together. Daphne felt secure in her own home, courageously accepting the inexorable nature of her illness. She died there on 25 July 2000.

Daphne left an indelible impression on all who knew her. She was a unique, truly remarkable woman who touched many lives.

She was perceived in varying ways. Because of her hesitancy of thought, some of her stories took quite a time to relate — but those with patience were richly rewarded. Young and old were thankful to have known Daphne and to have been able to talk with her, for she had great insight and knowledge.

Her giving and generous nature meant she derived great pleasure from seeing people succeed in their careers. She was interested in people and their families, and guided in the right direction when needed. She involved people. She had a remarkably active mind with a finely drawn imagination. She approached challenges with intensity, dedication and commitment.

Daphne mixed easily but at the same time she retained a certain dignity, a sense of the correct way of doing things, and a "Britishness" that could only be described as true patriotism. This was an inalienable part of her character.

Hers was a rich life filled with diverse experiences, a life that never just marked time. It is hard to put into words the rare being that was Daphne Pearson. Her unquestioning, instinctive courage has secured her richly deserved place in history. She always did what she thought was best, and trod a true path. She was so loved.

Audrey Jarvis
January 2001

321

Appendices

RAF/WAAF Ranks

RAF		WAAF
RAF		**WAAF**
Air Commodore	1940	Air Commandant
	1968	Air Commodore
Group Captain (Groupie)	1940	Air Officer
	1968	Group Captain
Wing Commander (Winco)	1940	Wing Officer
	1960s	Wing Commander
Squadron Leader	1940	Squadron Officer (Squoff)
	1960s	Squadron Leader
Flight Lieutenant	1940	Flying Officer
	1960s	Flight Lieutenant
Flying Officer	1940	Section Officer
	1960s	Flying Officer
Pilot Officer	1940	Assistant Section Officer
	1960s	Pilot Officer

In brackets: shortened slang terms

Acknowledgments

Helen Williams, typing and guidance with manuscript

Anne Latreille, transcription and guidance with postscript.

INDEX